190 VEGETARIAN
20-MINUTE RECIPES

190 VEGETARIAN
20-MINUTE RECIPES

A mouthwatering collection of simple, meat-free meals for the busy vegetarian cook, shown in over 170 fabulous photographs

CONTRIBUTING EDITOR: JENNI FLEETWOOD

southwater

This edition is published by Southwater,
an imprint of Anness Publishing Ltd,
Blaby Road, Wigston,
Leicestershire LE18 4SE

Email: info@anness.com

Web: www.southwaterbooks.com;
www.annesspublishing.com

If you like the images in this book and would like to
investigate using them for publishing, promotions or advertising,
please visit our website www.practicalpictures.com
for more information.

Publisher: Joanna Lorenz
Editorial Director: Helen Sudell
Editors: Elizabeth Woodland and Kate Eddison
Design: SMI and Diane Pullen
Cover Design: Nigel Partridge
Production Controller: Bessie Bai

© Anness Publishing Ltd 2011

Main front cover image shows Courgette Rissoles
– for recipe, see page 28

Previously published as part of a larger volume,
500 20-Minute Recipes

Ethical Trading Policy

At Anness Publishing we believe that business should be
conducted in an ethical and ecologically sustainable way, with
respect for the environment and a proper regard to the
replacement of the natural resources we employ.
As a publisher, we use a lot of wood pulp to make high-quality
paper for printing, and that wood commonly comes from spruce
trees. We are therefore currently growing more than 750,000
trees in three Scottish forest plantations: Berrymoss (130 hectares/
320 acres), West Touxhill (125 hectares/305 acres) and Deveron
Forest (75 hectares/185 acres). The forests we manage contain
more than 3.5 times the number of trees employed each year in
making paper for the books we manufacture.
Because of this ongoing ecological investment programme, you,
as our customer, can have the pleasure and reassurance of
knowing that a tree is being cultivated on your behalf to naturally
replace the materials used to make the book you are holding.
Our forestry programme is run in accordance with the UK
Woodland Assurance Scheme (UKWAS) and will be certified
by the internationally recognized Forest Stewardship Council
(FSC). The FSC is a non-government organization dedicated to
promoting responsible management of the world's forests.
Certification ensures forests are managed in an environmentally
sustainable and socially responsible way. For further information
about this scheme, go to www.annesspublishing.com/trees

Notes

Bracketed terms are intended for American readers.
For all recipes, quantities are given in both metric and imperial
measures and, where appropriate, in standard cups and spoons.
Follow one set of measures, but not a mixture, because they
are not interchangeable.

Standard spoon and cup measures are level.
1 tsp = 5ml, 1 tbsp = 15ml, 1 cup = 250ml/8fl oz.
Australian standard tablespoons are 20ml.
Australian readers should use 3 tsp in place of 1 tbsp for
measuring small quantities.
American pints are 16fl oz/2 cups. American readers should use
20fl oz/2.5 cups in place of 1 pint when measuring liquids.

Electric oven temperatures in this book are for conventional ovens.
When using a fan oven, the temperature will probably need to be
reduced by about 10–20°C/20–40°F. Since ovens vary, you should
check with your manufacturer's instruction book for guidance.

The nutritional analysis given for each recipe is calculated per
portion (i.e. serving or item), unless otherwise stated.

If the recipe gives a range, such as Serves 4–6, then the nutritional
analysis will be for the smaller portion size, i.e. 6 servings.

Measurements for sodium do not include salt added to taste.

Medium (US large) eggs are used unless otherwise stated.

Contents

Introduction

Twenty minutes isn't very long. You can easily spend that amount of time puzzling over a crossword clue, or trying to telephone a company determined to leave you on hold, or having a

cup of coffee in a busy restaurant. So can you cook a vegetarian meal in twenty minutes? Yes you can, and this book tells you how to do it.

Time: we never seem to have enough of it. Whether you are a student trying to balance study with a hectic social life, a single person trying to carve out a career, or a parent with a different but equally pressing set of priorities, time is a precious luxury. We're all riding the rollercoaster, rushing from home to work to home to sport to parents' evening to home to sleep. What you need in your repertoire are easy, no-fuss recipes: breakfasts you can blitz in a blender; lunches you can prepare and pack in next to no time; and suppers that raise your spirits without sapping any of the energy you have left at the end of the day. If you are entertaining, you want to do so in style, but without missing more than a few moments of your guests' company.

You can achieve these aims – after a fashion – by frequenting the ready-meal section of your favourite supermarket. Some days you'll do just that, but it is more rewarding and nutritious to serve something you've cooked yourself. When time is short, though, sometimes this can be

difficult to achieve. That's why this book takes a pragmatic approach to making vegetarian meals. Preparing your own vegetables is ideal, but if buying a bag of shake-it-out salad or some ready-trimmed beans means you can eat well and still get to your night class, go for it. Look out for quick-cook versions of favourite ingredients such as polenta and rice, and don't be afraid of mixing bought items like pesto with home-cooked pasta.

The aim of this book is to provide a wide-ranging selection of recipes that can be cooked in 20 minutes or less. That's assuming the cook is reasonably experienced. If you've never chopped an onion in your life, it is likely to take you a little longer. Efficient cooking is all about organization, so do read through your chosen recipe carefully, assemble your ingredients and give some thought to strategy. Recipe methods reflect this, but you need to work within the bounds of your own ability and the confines of your own kitchen. If a recipe calls for a slotted spoon and you need to rummage under the sink for one, you could lose valuable time, so be as

well prepared as possible. If you are inexperienced, the best way to start is by choosing the shortest recipes of 10 minutes or less, or opt for something that needs no cooking at all, such as a salad. Also, enlist aid when you can: getting a partner to line up ingredients can be a huge help.

Some of the recipes in this book require some advance preparation – for example soaking or chilling. The timeline at the top of the recipe will make it clear when this is required and there will probably be some mention of it in the recipe introduction, so do watch out for this. The recipes still won't take more than 20 minutes in all, but the preparation will be in stages and not all at the same time. Sometimes advance preparation can be a great advantage, such as when you want to get

some food for a dinner party done beforehand.

When you have extra time on your hands, consider making vegetable stock or a few tasty sauces that can be frozen for later use. Then, when you are in a rush, you'll have the means to make a simple, speedy meal that tastes great and is full of goodness. Putting all these tips into practice, and using the sumptuous recipes in this book, you'll be able to put quick vegetarian meals on the table time and time again.

Vitality Juice

The clue is in the name. This speedy juice really does put a spring in your step. Watercress has a slightly peppery flavour when eaten on its own, but blending it with pear, wheatgerm and yogurt tames the taste while boosting your morning energy levels.

Serves 4
25g/1oz watercress
1 large ripe pear
30ml/2 tbsp wheatgerm
150ml/¼ pint/⅔ cup natural (plain) yogurt
15ml/1 tbsp linseeds (flax seeds)
10ml/2 tsp lemon juice
mineral water (optional)
ice cubes

Preparation: 4 minutes; Cooking: 0 minutes

1 Roughly chop the watercress (you do not need to remove the tough stalks). Peel, core and roughly chop the pear.

2 Put the watercress and pear in a blender or food processor with the wheatgerm and blend until smooth. Scrape the mixture down from the side of the bowl, if necessary.

3 Add the yogurt, seeds and lemon juice and blend until combined. Thin with a little mineral water if too thick.

4 Put several ice cubes in the bottom of a tall glass. Fill the glass to just below the brim with the Vitality Juice, leaving enough room to decorate with a few sprigs of chopped watercress on top.

Variations
• *For a non-dairy version of this delicious, refreshing drink, use yogurt made from goat's milk, sheep's milk or soya.*
• *A large apple can be used instead of the pear.*
• *Linseeds are a very useful addition to this juice, as they have abundant levels of omega-3 and omega-6 fatty acids, which are good for strengthening immunity and easing digestive problems. However, they are not to everyone's taste, and three walnuts could be used instead.*

Pineapple, Ginger & Carrot Juice

You're never too busy for breakfast when you have recipes like this one in your repertoire. Ginger adds a zing to the sweet, scented mixture of fresh pineapple and carrot.

Makes 1 glass
½ small pineapple
25g/1oz fresh root ginger
1 carrot
ice cubes

Preparation: 5 minutes; Cooking: 0 minutes

1 Using a sharp knife, cut away the skin from the pineapple, then cut it into quarters and remove the core from each piece. Roughly slice the pineapple flesh and then chop into portions small enough to fit in the juicer.

2 Thinly peel the ginger, using a sharp knife or vegetable peeler, then chop the flesh roughly. Scrape or peel the carrot and cut it into rounds or chunks. Push the carrot, ginger and pineapple through a juicer and pour into a glass. Add ice cubes and serve.

Raspberry & Oatmeal Smoothie

Just a spoonful or so of oatmeal gives substance to this tangy, invigorating drink, providing slow-release carbohydrates to balance the fruit.

Makes 1 large glass
25ml/1½ tbsp medium oatmeal
150g/5oz/scant 1 cup raspberries
45ml/3 tbsp natural (plain) yogurt

Preparation: 2 minutes; Cooking: 0 minutes

1 Put the oats in a blender and add all but two or three of the raspberries, and about 30ml/2 tbsp of the yogurt. Blend until smooth, scraping down the side of the blender if necessary. Pour in 120ml/4fl oz/½ cup very cold water. Blend briefly. Pour the raspberry and oatmeal smoothie into a large glass, swirl in the remaining yogurt and top with the reserved raspberries.

Vitality Juice Energy 287kcal/1207kJ; Protein 17.8g; Carbohydrate 39.8g, of which sugars 31.2g; Fat 7.6g, of which saturates 1.6g; Cholesterol 2mg; Calcium 394mg; Fibre 8.8g; Sodium 144mg.
Pineapple Juice Energy 108kcal/462kJ; Protein 1.3g; Carbohydrate 26.1g, of which sugars 25.8g; Fat 0.6g, of which saturates 0.1g; Cholesterol 0mg; Calcium 55mg; Fibre 4.2g; Sodium 23mg.
Raspberry Smoothie Energy 186kcal/793kJ; Protein 7.5g; Carbohydrate 34.6g, of which sugars 16.4g; Fat 3.1g, of which saturates 0.4g; Cholesterol 1mg; Calcium 137mg; Fibre 5.4g; Sodium 51mg.

Muesli Smoothie

This divinely smooth drink has all the goodness but none of the lumpy bits.

Serves 2

50g/2oz/¼ cup ready-to-eat dried apricots

1 piece preserved stem ginger, plus 30ml/2 tbsp syrup from the ginger jar

40g/1½oz/scant ½ cup natural muesli (granola)

about 200ml/7fl oz/scant 1 cup semi-skimmed (low-fat) milk

Preparation: 4 minutes; Cooking: 0 minutes

1 Using a sharp knife, chop the dried apricots into slices or chunks. Chop the preserved ginger.

2 Put the apricots and ginger in a blender or food processor and add the syrup from the ginger jar with the muesli and milk. Process until smooth, adding more milk if necessary, to make a creamy drink. Serve in wide glasses.

Breakfast in a Glass

This energizing blend is simply bursting with goodness – just what you need when you wake up.

Serves 2

250g/9oz firm tofu

200g/7oz/1¾ cups strawberries

45ml/3 tbsp pumpkin or sunflower seeds, plus extra for sprinkling

30–45ml/2–3 tbsp clear honey

juice of 2 large oranges

juice of 1 lemon

Preparation: 5 minutes; Cooking: 0 minutes

1 Roughly chop the tofu, then hull and roughly chop the strawberries. Reserve a few strawberry chunks.

2 Put all the ingredients in a blender or food processor and blend until completely smooth, scraping the mixture down from the side of the bowl, if necessary. Pour into tumblers and sprinkle with extra seeds and strawberry chunks.

Big Breakfast

Easy to prepare, this energy-packed smoothie makes a great start to the day. Bananas and sesame seeds provide slow-release carbohydrate that will keep you going all morning.

Makes 2 glasses

½ mango

1 banana

1 large orange

30ml/2 tbsp wheatbran

15ml/1 tbsp sesame seeds

10–15ml/2–3 tsp honey

Preparation: 6 minutes; Cooking: 0 minutes

1 Using a small, sharp knife, skin the mango, then slice the flesh off the stone (pit). Peel the banana and break it into lengths, then place it in a blender or food processor with the mango.

2 Squeeze the juice from the orange and add to the blender or food processor along with the bran, sesame seeds and honey. Whizz until smooth and creamy, then pour into glasses.

Golden Wonder

Vitamin-rich and energizing, this drink is sure to set you up for the day. Passion fruit has a lovely tangy flavour which goes very well with banana.

Makes 1 large glass

2 passion fruit

2 yellow plums

1 small banana

about 15ml/1 tbsp lemon juice

Preparation: 3 minutes; Cooking: 0 minutes

1 Halve the passion fruit and, using a teaspoon, scoop the pulp into a blender or food processor. Using a small, sharp knife, halve and stone (pit) the plums and add to the blender or food processor.

2 Add the banana and lemon juice and blend the mixture until smooth, scraping the mixture down from the side of the bowl, if necessary. Pour into a large glass and check the sweetness. Add a little more lemon juice, if you like.

Muesli Smoothie Energy 204kcal/865kJ; Protein 6.6g; Carbohydrate 39.1g, of which sugars 28.8g; Fat 3.4g, of which saturates 1.4g; Cholesterol 6mg; Calcium 150mg; Fibre 3.1g; Sodium 97mg.
Breakfast in a Glass Energy 259kcal/1087kJ; Protein 13.3g; Carbohydrate 30.4g, of which sugars 28.2g; Fat 10.2g, of which saturates 1.1g; Cholesterol 0mg; Calcium 671mg; Fibre 1.8g; Sodium 19mg.
Big Breakfast Energy 172kcal/726kJ; Protein 4.9g; Carbohydrate 27.6g, of which sugars 23.1g; Fat 5.5g, of which saturates 0.9g; Cholesterol 0mg; Calcium 102mg; Fibre 8.5g; Sodium 11mg.
Golden Wonder Energy 108kcal/461kJ; Protein 2.1g; Carbohydrate 25.6g, of which sugars 23.7g; Fat 0.4g, of which saturates 0.1g; Cholesterol 0mg; Calcium 16mg; Fibre 2.8g; Sodium 8mg.

Vanilla Caffe Latte

This luxurious vanilla and chocolate version of the classic coffee drink can be served at any time of day topped with whipped cream. Serve in mugs or heatproof glasses, with cinnamon sticks to stir and flavour the coffee.

Serves 2
700ml/24fl oz/scant 3 cups milk
250ml/8fl oz/1 cup espresso or
 very strong coffee
45ml/3 tbsp vanilla sugar, plus
 extra to taste
115g/4oz dark (bittersweet)
 chocolate, grated

Preparation: 3 minutes; Cooking: 8 minutes

1 Pour the milk into a small pan and bring to the boil, then remove from the heat.

2 Mix the espresso or very strong coffee with 500ml/16fl oz/ 2 cups of the boiled milk in a large heatproof jug (pitcher). Sweeten with vanilla sugar to taste.

3 Return the remaining boiled milk in the pan to the heat and add the 45ml/3 tbsp vanilla sugar. Stir constantly until dissolved. Bring to the boil, then reduce the heat.

4 Add the dark chocolate and continue to heat, stirring constantly until all the chocolate has melted and the mixture is smooth and glossy.

5 Pour the chocolate milk into the jug of coffee and whisk thoroughly. Serve in mugs or glasses.

Variation
The fun thing about this drink is that the taste can be varied, depending on what type of chocolate you buy. Orange, peppermint, hazelnut, almond – the choice is as wide as the selection on the supermarket shelf. Echo the coffee flavour with espresso chocolate or try a more unusual offering, such as pistachio chocolate or a crème brûlée flavour. Grate more chocolate on top for extra pleasure.

Banana & Maple Flip

This satisfying drink is packed with so much goodness that it makes a complete breakfast in a glass. It takes only moments to make so is the perfect way to start a busy day.

Serves 1
1 small banana, peeled
 and halved
50ml/2fl oz/¼ cup thick Greek
 (US strained plain) yogurt
1 egg
30ml/2 tbsp maple syrup

Preparation: 4 minutes; Cooking: 0 minutes

1 Put the peeled and halved banana, thick Greek yogurt, egg and maple syrup in a food processor or blender. Add 30ml/2 tbsp chilled water or an ice cube.

2 Process the ingredients constantly for about 2 minutes, or until the mixture turns a really pale, creamy colour and has a nice frothy texture. Pour the drink into a tall, chilled glass and serve immediately.

Warning
The very young, the elderly and pregnant women are advised against consuming raw eggs or drinks containing raw eggs.

Frothy Hot Chocolate

Make this with the best chocolate you can afford, whisked in hot milk until really frothy. Use an electric frother for best results.

Serves 4
1 litre/1¾ pints/4 cups milk
1 vanilla pod (bean)
50–115g/2–4oz dark
 (bittersweet) chocolate, grated

Preparation: 3 minutes; Cooking: 4 minutes

1 Pour the milk into a pan. Split the vanilla pod lengthways using a sharp knife to reveal the seeds, and add it to the milk; the vanilla seeds and the pod will flavour the milk. Add the chocolate. The amount to use depends on personal taste – start with a smaller amount if you are unsure of the flavour and taste at the beginning of step 2, adding more if necessary.

2 Heat the chocolate milk gently, stirring until all the chocolate has melted and the mixture is smooth, then whisk with a wire whisk until the mixture boils. Remove the vanilla pod from the pan and divide the drink among four mugs or heatproof glasses. Serve immediately.

Variation
You could use Mexican chocolate, which is flavoured with almonds, cinnamon and vanilla, and sweetened with sugar. All the ingredients are crushed together in a special mortar, and heated over coals. The powdered mixture is then shaped into discs, which can be bought in specialist stores.

Vanilla Caffe Latte Energy 545Kcal/2299kJ; Protein 15g; Carbohydrate 77g, of which sugars 76g; Fat 22g, of which saturates 13g; Cholesterol 24mg; Calcium 445mg; Fibre 1.4g; Sodium 200mg.
Banana and Maple Flip Energy 376Kcal/1573kJ; Protein 12g; Carbohydrate 58g, of which sugars 52g; Fat 12g, of which saturates 5g; Cholesterol 240mg; Calcium 141mg; Fibre 0.9g; Sodium 100mg.
Frothy Hot Chocolate Energy 223Kcal/942kJ; Protein 10g; Carbohydrate 25g, of which sugars 25g; Fat 10g, of which saturates 6g; Cholesterol 16mg; Calcium 307mg; Fibre 0.5g; Sodium 100mg.

Thick Banana Smoothie with Rich Chocolate Sauce

The secret of a good smoothie is to serve it ice-cold and whizzing it up with ice is the perfect way to ensure this. Keep an ice tray of frozen orange juice at the ready for drinks like these.

Serves 2 generously
For the smoothie
3 ripe bananas
200ml/7fl oz/scant 1 cup natural (plain) yogurt

30ml/2 tbsp mild honey
350ml/12fl oz/1½ cups orange juice ice cubes, crushed

For the hot chocolate sauce
175g/6oz plain (semisweet) chocolate with more than 60% cocoa solids
60ml/4 tbsp water
15ml/1 tbsp golden (light corn) syrup
15g/½oz/1 tbsp butter

Preparation: 5 minutes; Cooking: 10–12 minutes

1 Peel and chop the bananas, put them in a bowl, then mash them with a fork.

2 For the sauce, break up the chocolate and put into a bowl over a pan of barely simmering water. Leave undisturbed for 10 minutes until the chocolate has melted, then add the water, syrup and butter and stir until smooth.

3 Place the mashed bananas, yogurt, honey and orange ice cubes in a blender or food processor and blend until smooth, operating the machine in short bursts or pulsing for best results.

4 Pour into large, tall glasses, then pour in some chocolate sauce from a height. The sauce will swirl around the glasses to give a marbled effect. Serve with long-handled spoons.

Cook's Tip
Pouring chocolate sauce like this cools it slightly on the way down, so that it thickens on contact with the cold smoothie.

Cantaloupe Melon Salad

Lightly caramelized ripe strawberries look pretty and taste divine in this simplest of salads. Serve it for a special occasion brunch.

Serves 4
115g/4oz/1 cup strawberries
15ml/1 tbsp icing (confectioners') sugar, plus extra for dusting
½ cantaloupe melon

Preparation: 3 minutes; Cooking: 4–5 minutes

1 Preheat the grill (broiler) to high. Hull the strawberries and cut them in half. Arrange the fruit in a single layer, cut side up, on a baking sheet or in an ovenproof dish and dust with the icing sugar.

2 Grill (broil) the strawberries for 4–5 minutes, or until the sugar starts to bubble and turn golden.

3 Meanwhile, scoop out the seeds from the half melon using a spoon. Using a sharp knife, remove the skin, then cut the flesh into wedges. Arrange the melon wedges attractively on a serving plate and sprinkle the lightly caramelized strawberries on top. Dust the salad with icing sugar and serve immediately.

Zingy Papaya Fruit Salad

This refreshing, fruity salad makes a lovely light breakfast, perfect for the summer months when meals tend to be light.

Serves 4
2 large ripe papayas
juice of 1 fresh lime
2 pieces preserved stem ginger, finely sliced

Preparation: 5 minutes; Cooking: 0 minutes

1 Cut the papayas in half lengthways. Scoop out the seeds, using a teaspoon. With a sharp knife, cut the flesh into neat, thin slices. Arrange the papaya slices on a platter. Squeeze the lime juice over the papaya and sprinkle with the sliced stem ginger. Serve immediately.

Smoothie Energy 901kcal/3790kJ; Protein 13.2g; Carbohydrate 148.1g, of which sugars 142.2g; Fat 32.5g, of which saturates 19.4g; Cholesterol 23mg; Calcium 253mg; Fibre 4.9g; Sodium 176mg.
Cantaloupe Melon Energy 34kcal/144kJ; Protein 0.7g; Carbohydrate 8g, of which sugars 8g; Fat 0.1g, of which saturates 0g; Cholesterol 0mg; Calcium 21mg; Fibre 1.1g; Sodium 8mg.
Zingy Papaya Energy 112kcal/475kJ; Protein 1.6g; Carbohydrate 27.3g, of which sugars 27.3g; Fat 0.3g, of which saturates 0g; Cholesterol 0mg; Calcium 72mg; Fibre 6.8g; Sodium 16mg.

Cranachan Crunch

This tasty breakfast dish is based on a traditional Scottish recipe. The toasted cereal tastes delicious with yogurt and a generous drizzle of heather honey.

Serves 4

75g/3oz crunchy oat cereal
600ml/1 pint/2½ cups Greek
(US strained plain) yogurt
250g/9oz/1½ cups raspberries

Preparation: 2 minutes; Cooking: 3–4 minutes

1 Preheat the grill (broiler) to high. Spread the oat cereal on a baking sheet and place under the hot grill for 3–4 minutes until lightly toasted, stirring regularly. Set aside to cool.

2 When the oat cereal has cooled completely, fold it into the Greek yogurt, then gently fold in 200g/7oz/generous 1 cup of the raspberries, being careful not to crush the berries too much.

3 Spoon the yogurt mixture into four serving glasses or dishes, top with the remaining raspberries and serve immediately.

Classic Porridge

Porridge remains a favourite way to start the day, especially on chilly winter mornings.

Serves 4

750ml/1¼ pints/3 cups water
115g/4oz/1 cup rolled oats
good pinch of salt

Preparation: 1–2 minutes; Cooking: 7–8 minutes

1 Put the water, rolled oats and salt into a heavy pan and bring to the boil over a medium heat, stirring with a wooden spatula to prevent sticking.

2 Simmer for about 5 minutes, stirring frequently, then spoon into bowls.

3 Serve hot with cold milk and extra salt, if required.

Cinnamon Toast

This is an old-fashioned snack that is warming and comforting on a cold autumnal morning. Cinnamon toast is perfect with a spicy hot chocolate drink or with a few slices of fresh fruit such as peaches, plums, nectarines or mango.

Serves 2

75g/3oz/6 tbsp butter, softened
10ml/2 tsp ground cinnamon
30ml/2 tbsp caster (superfine)
sugar, plus extra to serve
4 slices bread
prepared fresh fruit

Preparation: 2 minutes; Cooking: 2–3 minutes

1 Place the softened butter in a bowl. Beat with a spoon until soft and creamy, then mix in the ground cinnamon and most of the sugar.

2 Toast the bread on both sides. Spread with the butter and sprinkle with a little remaining sugar. Serve at once, with pieces of fresh fruit, if you like.

Variations
You can use any type of bread for cinnamon toast. Wholewheat or granary adds a nuttiness that goes well with fruit like apricots, peaches or mangoes. A fruit loaf or halved hot cross buns would taste delicious, and for a seasonal treat around Christmas time, try this with panettone. For a special treat, serve a generous dollop of thick, creamy yogurt on the side, or a spoonful of crème fraîche.

Cook's Tip
To round off this winter warmer, serve a quick cardamom hot chocolate with the cinnamon toast. Put 900ml/1½ pints/ 3¾ cups milk in a pan with two bruised cardamom pods and bring to the boil. Add 200g/7oz plain (semisweet) chocolate and whisk until melted. Using a slotted spoon, remove the cardamom pods just before serving.

Cranachan Crunch Energy 222kcal/935kJ; Protein 10.1g; Carbohydrate 23g, of which sugars 13.3g; Fat 10.7g, of which saturates 6.7g; Cholesterol 21mg; Calcium 250mg; Fibre 3g; Sodium 236mg.
Classic Porridge Energy 460kcal/1952kJ; Protein 14.4g; Carbohydrate 83.6g, of which sugars 0g; Fat 10g, of which saturates 0g; Cholesterol 0mg; Calcium 64mg; Fibre 8g; Sodium 1216mg.
Cinnamon Toast Energy 461kcal/1921kJ; Protein 4.7g; Carbohydrate 41.6g, of which sugars 17.3g; Fat 31.8g, of which saturates 19.6g; Cholesterol 80mg; Calcium 72mg; Fibre 0.8g; Sodium 499mg.

Griddled Tomatoes on Soda Bread

Nothing could be simpler than this basic brunch dish, transformed into something special by adding a drizzle of olive oil, balsamic vinegar and shavings of Parmesan cheese to griddled tomatoes and serving them on toast.

Serves 4
olive oil, for brushing and drizzling
6 tomatoes, thickly sliced
4 thick slices soda bread
balsamic vinegar, for drizzling
salt and ground black pepper
shavings of Parmesan cheese,
   to serve

Preparation: 2 minutes; Cooking: 4–6 minutes

1 Brush a griddle pan with olive oil and heat. Add the tomato slices and cook for 4–6 minutes, turning once, until softened and slightly blackened. Alternatively, heat a grill (broiler) to high and line the rack with foil. Grill (broil) the tomato slices for 4–6 minutes, turning once, until softened.

2 While the tomatoes are cooking, lightly toast the soda bread. Place the tomatoes on top of the toast and drizzle each portion with a little olive oil and vinegar. Season to taste and serve immediately with thin shavings of Parmesan.

Variation
A dish like this one tastes perfect on its own, but if you prefer something slightly more substantial, add slices of bacon, grilled (broiled) until crisp, or some herby sausage. When cooking the sausage, don't prick it first, as this allows juices to flow out and tends to make the sausage dry. If you grill the sausage under low to medium heat, and turn it often, it will be unlikely to burst.

Cook's Tip
Using a griddle pan reduces the amount of oil required for cooking the tomatoes and gives them a barbecued flavour. The ridges on the pan brand the tomatoes, which gives them an attractive appearance.

Mushrooms on Spicy Toast

Dry-panning is a quick way of cooking mushrooms that makes the most of their flavour. It works well with large, flat mushrooms. The juices run when they are heated, so they become really moist and tender.

Serves 4
8–12 large flat field (portabello)
   mushrooms
50g/1oz/2 tbsp butter
5ml/1 tsp curry paste
salt
4 slices thickly sliced white bread,
   toasted, to serve

Preparation: 2–3 minutes; Cooking: 4–5 minutes

1 Preheat the oven to 200°C/400°F/Gas 6. Peel the field mushrooms, if necessary, and remove the stalks. Heat a dry frying pan until very hot.

2 Place the mushrooms in the hot frying pan, with the gills on top. Using half the butter, add a piece the size of a hazelnut to each one, then sprinkle all the mushrooms lightly with salt. Cook over a medium heat until the butter begins to bubble and the mushrooms are juicy and tender.   ·

3 Meanwhile, mix the remaining butter with the curry paste. Spread on the toasted bread. Bake in the oven for 10 minutes, pile the mushrooms on top and serve.

Variations
Using a flavoured butter makes these mushrooms even more special. Try one of the following.
• Herb butter Mix softened butter with chopped fresh herbs such as parsley and thyme, or marjoram and chopped chives.
• Olive butter Mix softened butter with diced green olives and spring onions (scallions).
• Tomato butter Mix softened butter with sun-dried tomato purée (paste).
• Garlic butter Mix softened butter with finely chopped garlic.
• Pepper and paprika butter Mix softened butter with 2.5ml/½ tsp paprika and 2.5ml/½ tsp black pepper.

Griddled Tomatoes Energy 178kcal/751kJ; Protein 4.2g; Carbohydrate 26.3g, of which sugars 6.9g; Fat 7g, of which saturates 1g; Cholesterol 0mg; Calcium 66mg; Fibre 2.7g; Sodium 175mg.
Mushrooms Energy 230kcal/966kJ; Protein 6.1g; Carbohydrate 25.1g, of which sugars 1.6g; Fat 12.5g, of which saturates 6.7g; Cholesterol 27mg; Calcium 63mg; Fibre 1.9g; Sodium 341mg.

Chilled Tomato Soup with Rocket Pesto

This soup takes hardly any time to make, but must be chilled, so bear that in mind when planning your menu. Whizz it up when you wake, and make the pesto just before serving.

Serves 4
225g/8oz cherry tomatoes, halved
225g/8oz baby plum
  tomatoes, halved
225g/8oz vine-ripened
  tomatoes, halved
2 shallots, roughly chopped

25ml/1½ tbsp sun-dried tomato
  purée (paste)
600ml/1 pint/2½ cups
  vegetable stock
salt and ground black pepper
ice cubes, to serve

For the rocket pesto
15g/½ oz rocket
  (arugula) leaves
75ml/5 tbsp olive oil
15g/½ oz/2 tbsp pine nuts
1 garlic clove
25g/1oz/⅓ cup freshly grated
  Parmesan or Romano cheese

Preparation: 10 minutes; Cooking: 4–5 minutes; Chilling ahead

1 Purée all the tomatoes and the shallots in a food processor or blender. Add the sun-dried tomato paste and process until smooth. Press the purée through a sieve (strainer) into a pan.

2 Add the vegetable stock and heat gently for 4–5 minutes. Season well. Pour into a bowl, leave to cool, then chill for at least 4 hours.

3 For the rocket pesto, put the rocket, oil, pine nuts and garlic in a food processor or blender and process to form a paste. Transfer to a bowl and stir in the Parmesan cheese. (This can also be prepared using a mortar and pestle. Pound the rocket leaves, chopped pine nuts and crushed garlic together, then add the oil a little at a time, continuing to pound the mixture. Add the Parmesan and work it in.)

4 Ladle the soup into bowls and add a few ice cubes to each. Spoon some of the rocket pesto into the centre of each portion and serve.

Gazpacho

Probably the most famous chilled soup in the world, this originated in Spain but now appears on menus everywhere. It is perfect for a summer lunch.

Serves 6
900g/2lb ripe tomatoes, peeled
  and seeded
1 cucumber, peeled and
  roughly chopped
2 red (bell) peppers, seeded and
  roughly chopped
2 garlic cloves, crushed
1 large onion, roughly chopped
30ml/2 tbsp white wine vinegar
120ml/4fl oz/½ cup olive oil

250g/9oz/4½ cups fresh
  white breadcrumbs
450ml/¾ pint/scant 2 cups
  iced water
salt and ground black pepper
ice cubes, to serve

For the garnish
30–45ml/2–3 tbsp olive oil
4 thick slices bread, crusts
  removed, cut into small cubes
2 tomatoes, peeled, seeded and
  finely diced
1 small green (bell) pepper,
  seeded and finely diced
1 small onion, very finely sliced
a small bunch of fresh flat leaf
  parsley, chopped

Preparation: 12 minutes; Cooking: 5–6 minutes; Chilling ahead

1 In a large bowl, mix the tomatoes, cucumber, peppers, garlic and onion. Stir in the vinegar, oil, breadcrumbs and water until well mixed.

2 Purée the mixture in a food processor or blender until almost smooth, and pour into a large bowl. Stir in salt and pepper to taste and chill for at least 4 hours.

3 To make the garnish, heat the oil in a frying pan and add the bread cubes.

4 Fry over a medium heat for 5–6 minutes, stirring occasionally to brown evenly. Lift out the cubes with a slotted spoon, drain on kitchen paper and put into a small bowl. Place the remaining garnishing ingredients in separate bowls or on a serving plate.

5 Ladle the gazpacho into bowls and add ice cubes to each portion. Serve at once with the garnishing ingredients.

Tomato Soup Energy 218kcal/902kJ; Protein 4.8g; Carbohydrate 7.5g, of which sugars 7.2g; Fat 19g, of which saturates 3.6g; Cholesterol 6mg; Calcium 100mg; Fibre 2.2g; Sodium 104mg.
Gazpacho Energy 412kcal/1730kJ; Protein 9.1g; Carbohydrate 55.6g, of which sugars 14.7g; Fat 18.6g, of which saturates 2.6g; Cholesterol 0mg; Calcium 109mg; Fibre 5g; Sodium 431mg.

Fresh Tomato Soup

The combination of intensely flavoured sun-ripened and fresh tomatoes needs little embellishment in this tasty Italian soup.

Serves 6
1.3–1.6kg/3–3½lb ripe tomatoes
400ml/14fl oz/1⅔ cups vegetable stock
45ml/3 tbsp sun-dried tomato purée (paste)
30–45ml/2–3 tbsp balsamic vinegar
10–15ml/2–3 tsp sugar
a small handful of fresh basil leaves, plus extra to garnish
salt and ground black pepper
toasted cheese croûtes and crème fraîche, to serve

Preparation: 5–6 minutes; Cooking: 14 minutes

1 Plunge the tomatoes into boiling water for 30 seconds, then refresh in cold water. Peel off the skins and cut the tomatoes into quarters.

2 Put the tomatoes in a large pan and pour over the vegetable stock. Bring just to the boil, reduce the heat, cover and simmer gently for 10 minutes until the tomatoes are pulpy.

3 Stir in the tomato purée, vinegar, sugar and basil. Season with salt and pepper, then cook gently, stirring, for 2 minutes.

4 Process the soup in a blender or food processor, then return to a clean pan and reheat gently. Serve in bowls, topped with one or two toasted cheese croûtes and a spoonful of crème fraîche, garnished with basil leaves.

Cook's Tips
• Use a sharp knife to cut a cross in the base of each tomato before plunging it into the boiling water. The skin will then peel back easily from the crosses.
• To make the toasted cheese croûtes, slice a loaf of French bread thinly. Spread out the slices in a grill (broiler) pan and top each with finely grated Cheddar or Parmesan cheese. Grill (broil) until the cheese has melted and browned slightly.

Cauliflower Cream Soup

This delicately flavoured, thick winter soup is enriched at the last minute with chopped hard-boiled eggs and crème fraîche. Use broccoli in place of the cauliflower to equal effect.

Serves 4
1 cauliflower, cut into large pieces
1 large onion, roughly chopped
1 large garlic clove, chopped
bouquet garni
5ml/1 tsp ground coriander
pinch of mustard powder
900ml/1½ pints/3¾ cups vegetable stock
5–10ml/1–2 tsp cornflour (cornstarch)
150ml/¼ pint/⅔ cup milk
45ml/3 tbsp crème fraîche
2 eggs, hard-boiled and roughly chopped
15ml/1 tbsp chopped fresh coriander (cilantro)
salt and ground black pepper

Preparation: 5 minutes; Cooking: 13–15 minutes

1 Place the cauliflower in a large pan with the onion, garlic, bouquet garni, coriander, mustard, salt and pepper and stock. Simmer for 10–15 minutes until the cauliflower is tender. Remove from the heat and leave to cool slightly.

2 Remove the garlic and bouquet garni, then blend the cauliflower and onion with some of the cooking liquid in a food processor, or press through a sieve (strainer) for a really smooth result. Return to the pan along with the rest of the liquid.

3 Blend the cornflour with a little of the milk, then add to the soup with the rest of the milk. Return to the heat and cook until thickened, stirring all the time. Season to taste and, just before serving, turn off the heat and blend in the crème fraîche. Stir in the chopped egg and coriander and serve at once.

Cook's Tip
Garlic croûtons would make a delicious accompaniment. Cut white bread into cubes. Heat a mixture of butter and oil in a frying pan, fry 1 crushed garlic clove gently to flavour it, then remove the garlic and fry the bread cubes until crisp.

Fresh Tomato Soup Energy 52Kcal/225kJ; Protein 1.9g; Carbohydrate 10.4g, of which sugars 10.4g; Fat 0.7g, of which saturates 0.2g; Cholesterol 0mg; Calcium 19mg; Fibre 2.4g; Sodium 38mg.
Cauliflower Soup Energy 169kcal/711kJ; Protein 7.4g; Carbohydrate 27.7g, of which sugars 10.8g; Fat 4g, of which saturates 1.1g; Cholesterol 3mg; Calcium 111mg; Fibre 4g; Sodium 55mg.

Stilton & Watercress Soup

A good creamy Stilton cheese and plenty of peppery watercress bring maximum flavour to this rich, smooth soup, which is superlative in small portions and very quick to prepare. It is ideal for a dinner party.

Serves 4–6
600ml/1 pint/2½ cups
   vegetable stock
225g/8oz watercress
150g/5oz Stilton or other
   blue cheese
150ml/¼ pint/⅔ cup single
   (light) cream

Preparation: 6 minutes; Cooking: 8 minutes

1 Pour the stock into a pan and bring almost to the boil. Remove and discard any very large stalks from the watercress. Add the watercress to the pan and simmer gently for 2–3 minutes, until tender.

2 Crumble the cheese into the pan and simmer for 1 minute more, until the cheese has started to melt. Process the soup in a blender or food processor, in batches if necessary, until very smooth. Return the soup to the pan.

3 Stir in the cream and check the seasoning. The soup will probably not need any extra salt, as the blue cheese is already quite salty. Heat the soup gently, without boiling, then ladle it into warm bowls.

Variations
• Rocket (arugula) can be used as an alternative to watercress – both leaves are an excellent source of iron. When choosing any salad leaves, look for crisp, fresh leaves and reject any wilted or discoloured greens.
• Stilton is the classic cheese for this soup, but there are plenty of other options. Gorgonzola and Roquefort can be used, but they have punchy flavours and you may need to use slightly less. Milder options include Bleu de Bresse, Irish Cashel Blue or Cambozola.

Japanese-style Noodle Soup

This delicate, fragrant soup, flavoured with a hint of chilli, makes a delicious light lunch or first course.

Serves 4
45ml/3 tbsp miso
200g/7oz/scant 2 cups udon
   noodles, soba noodles or
   Chinese noodles
30ml/2 tbsp sake or dry sherry
15ml/1 tbsp rice or
   wine vinegar
45ml/3 tbsp Japanese soy sauce
115g/4oz asparagus tips or
   mangetouts (snow peas), thinly
   sliced diagonally
50g/2oz/scant 1 cup shiitake
   mushrooms, stalks removed and
   thinly sliced
1 carrot, sliced into julienne strips
3 spring onions (scallions), thinly
   sliced diagonally
salt and ground black pepper
5ml/1 tsp dried chilli flakes,
   to serve

Preparation: 8 minutes; Cooking: 10 minutes

1 Bring 1 litre/1¾ pints/4 cups water to the boil in a large pan. Pour 150ml/¼ pint/⅔ cup of the boiling water over the miso and stir until dissolved, then set aside.

2 Meanwhile, bring another large pan of lightly salted water to the boil, add the noodles and cook according to the packet instructions until just tender.

3 Drain the noodles in a colander. Rinse under cold running water, then drain again.

4 Add the sake or sherry, rice or wine vinegar and soy sauce to the boiling water remaining in the first pan. Boil gently for 3 minutes then reduce the heat to a simmer and stir in the miso mixture.

5 Add the asparagus or mangetouts, mushrooms, carrot and spring onions, and simmer for about 2 minutes until the vegetables are just tender. Season to taste.

6 Divide the noodles among four warm bowls and pour the soup over the top. Serve immediately, sprinkled with the dried chilli flakes.

Stilton and Watercress Energy 162Kcal/671kJ; Protein 8g; Carbohydrate 1g, of which sugars 1g; Fat 14g, of which saturates 9g; Cholesterol 38mg; Calcium 169mg; Fibre 0.6g; Sodium 400mg.
Noodle Soup Energy 254kcal/1076kJ; Protein 10.2g; Carbohydrate 48.1g, of which sugars 4.9g; Fat 3.6g, of which saturates 0.1g; Cholesterol 0mg; Calcium 37mg; Fibre 3.4g; Sodium 814mg.

Egg Flower Soup

This simple, healthy soup is flavoured with fresh root ginger and Chinese five-spice powder. It is quick and delicious and can be made at the last minute.

Serves 4
1.2 litres/2 pints/5 cups fresh
  vegetable stock
10ml/2 tsp peeled, grated fresh
  root ginger
10ml/2 tsp light soy sauce
5ml/1 tsp sesame oil
5ml/1 tsp Chinese five-spice
  powder
15–30ml/1–2 tbsp cornflour
  (cornstarch)
2 eggs
salt and ground black pepper
1 spring onion (scallion), very finely
  sliced diagonally and 15ml/
  1 tbsp roughly chopped
  coriander (cilantro) or flat leaf
  parsley, to garnish

Preparation: 3–4 minutes; Cooking: 16 minutes

1 Put the vegetable stock into a large pan with the ginger, soy sauce, oil and five-spice powder. Bring to the boil and allow to simmer gently for about 10 minutes.

2 Blend the cornflour in a measuring jug (cup) with 60–75ml/ 4–5 tbsp water and stir into the stock. Cook, stirring constantly, until slightly thickened. Season to taste with salt and pepper.

3 In a jug, beat the eggs together with 30ml/2 tbsp cold water until the mixture becomes frothy.

4 Bring the soup back just to the boil and drizzle in the egg mixture, stirring vigorously with chopsticks until the egg begins to solidify. Serve at once, sprinkled with the sliced spring onions and chopped coriander or parsley.

> **Cook's Tip**
> This soup is a good way of using up leftover egg yolks or whites, which have been stored in the freezer and then thawed. When adding the egg to the soup, use a jug with a fine spout to form a very thin drizzle.

Hot & Sweet Vegetable Soup

This soothing, nutritious soup takes only minutes to make as the spinach and silken tofu are simply placed in bowls and covered with the richly flavoured hot vegetable stock.

Serves 4
1.2 litres/2 pints/5 cups
  vegetable stock
5–10ml/1–2 tsp Thai red
  curry paste
2 kaffir lime leaves, torn
40g/1½ oz/3 tbsp palm sugar or
  light muscovado (brown) sugar
30ml/2 tbsp soy sauce
juice of 1 lime
1 carrot, cut into thin batons
50g/2oz baby spinach leaves, any
  coarse stalks removed
225g/8oz block silken tofu, diced

Preparation: 4 minutes; Cooking: 7–12 minutes

1 Heat the stock in a large pan, then add the red curry paste. Stir constantly over a medium heat until the paste has dissolved. Add the lime leaves, sugar and soy sauce and bring to the boil. Add the lime juice and carrot to the pan. Reduce the heat and simmer for 5–10 minutes. Place the spinach and tofu in four individual serving bowls and pour the hot vegetable stock on top to serve.

Miso Broth with Mushrooms

Shiitake mushrooms give this soup superb flavour.

Serves 4
1.2 litres/2 pints/5 cups boiling
  water
3 tbsp light miso paste
3 fresh shiitake mushrooms, sliced
115g/4 oz tofu, diced
1 spring onion (scallion), green
  part only, sliced

Preparation: 4 minutes; Cooking: 5 minutes

1 Mix the boiling water and miso in a pan. Add the mushrooms and simmer for 5 minutes. Divide the tofu among four warmed soup bowls, ladle in the soup, scatter with sliced spring onions and serve.

Egg Flower Soup Energy 58kcal/244kJ; Protein 3.3g; Carbohydrate 3.8g, of which sugars 0.3g; Fat 3.6g, of which saturates 0.9g; Cholesterol 95mg; Calcium 16mg; Fibre 0g; Sodium 304mg.
Hot & Sweet Soup Energy 105Kcal/439kJ; Protein 5.3g; Carbohydrate 13.2g, of which sugars 12.8g; Fat 3.8g, of which saturates 0.5g; Cholesterol 0mg; Calcium 320mg; Fibre 0.7g; Sodium 559mg.
Miso Broth Energy 25kcal/103kJ; Protein 2.4g; Carbohydrate 2.6g, of which sugars 2.4g; Fat 0.6g, of which saturates 0.1g; Cholesterol 0mg; Calcium 107mg; Fibre 1.6g; Sodium 882mg.

Tapas of Almonds, Olives & Cheese

Serving a few choice nibbles with drinks is the perfect way to get an evening off to a good start, and when you can get everything ready ahead of time, life's easier all round.

Serves 6–8
For the marinated olives
2.5ml/½ tsp coriander seeds
2.5ml/½ tsp fennel seeds
2 garlic cloves, crushed
5ml/1 tsp chopped fresh rosemary
10ml/2 tsp chopped fresh parsley
15ml/1 tbsp sherry vinegar
30ml/2 tbsp olive oil
115g/4oz/⅔ cup black olives
115g/4oz/⅔ cup green olives

For the marinated cheese
150g/5oz Manchego or other firm cheese
90ml/6 tbsp olive oil
15ml/1 tbsp white wine vinegar
5ml/1 tsp black peppercorns
1 garlic clove, sliced
fresh thyme or tarragon sprigs
fresh flat leaf parsley or tarragon sprigs, to garnish (optional)

For the salted almonds
1.5ml/¼ tsp cayenne pepper
30ml/2 tbsp sea salt
25g/1oz/2 tbsp butter
60ml/4 tbsp olive oil
200g/7oz/1¾ cups blanched almonds

Preparation: 10–15 minutes; Cooking: 5 minutes; Make ahead

1 To make the marinated olives, crush the coriander and fennel seeds in a mortar with a pestle. Work in the garlic, then add the rosemary, parsley, vinegar and olive oil. Mix well. Put the olives in a small bowl and pour over the marinade. Cover with clear film (plastic wrap) and chill for up to 1 week.

2 To make the marinated cheese, cut the Manchego or other firm cheese into bitesize pieces, removing any rind, and put in a small bowl. Combine the oil, vinegar, peppercorns, garlic, thyme or tarragon and pour over the cheese. Cover with clear film and chill for up to 3 days.

3 To make the salted almonds, combine the cayenne pepper and salt in a bowl. Melt the butter with the oil in a frying pan. Add the almonds and fry them, stirring, for 5 minutes. Tip the almonds into the salt mixture and toss until they are coated. Leave to cool, then store in an airtight container for up to 1 week. Serve the almonds, olives, and cheese in separate dishes.

Guacamole

Serve this tangy avocado dip with tortilla chips or crudités as scoops.

Serves 4
2 ripe avocados, peeled
2 tomatoes, peeled, seeded and chopped

6 spring onions (scallions), finely chopped
30ml/2 tbsp fresh lime juice
15ml/1 tbsp chopped fresh coriander (cilantro)
salt and ground black pepper
fresh coriander (cilantro) sprigs to garnish

Preparation: 5 minutes; Cooking: 0 minutes

1 Mash the avocado flesh with a fork and add the remaining ingredients. Season with salt and pepper and mix well. Garnish with sprigs of coriander.

Hummus

This classic Middle Eastern dish is made from cooked chickpeas, ground to a paste and flavoured with garlic, lemon juice, tahini, olive oil and cumin. Serve with pitta wedges or on toast fingers. Hummus also makes a good filling for hollowed-out cocktail tomatoes.

Serves 4–6
400g/14oz can chickpeas, drained
60ml/4 tbsp tahini
2–3 garlic cloves, chopped
juice of ½–1 lemon
cayenne pepper to taste
small pinch to 1.5ml/¼ tsp ground cumin, or more to taste
salt and ground black pepper

Preparation: 5 minutes; Cooking: 0 minutes

1 Using a potato masher or food processor, coarsely mash the chickpeas. If you prefer a smoother purée, process them in a food processor or blender until smooth.

2 Mix the tahini into the chickpeas, then stir in the garlic, lemon juice, cayenne, cumin and salt and pepper to taste. If needed, add a little water. Serve at room temperature.

Tapas Energy 383kcal/1580kJ; Protein 10.3g; Carbohydrate 1.8g, of which sugars 1.1g; Fat 36.8g, of which saturates 8.9g; Cholesterol 25mg; Calcium 217mg; Fibre 2.7g; Sodium 1051mg.
Guacamole Energy 156kcal/645kJ; Protein 2.1g; Carbohydrate 3.7g, of which sugars 2.5g; Fat 14.7g, of which saturates 3.1g; Cholesterol 0mg; Calcium 26mg; Fibre 3.5g; Sodium 11mg.
Hummus Energy 140kcal/586kJ; Protein 6.9g; Carbohydrate 11.2g, of which sugars 0.4g; Fat 7.8g, of which saturates 1.1g; Cholesterol 0mg; Calcium 97mg; Fibre 3.6g; Sodium 149mg.

Chopped Eggs & Onions

Quick and easy to make, this is a speedy lunch. You could even pack it up and take it to work, although the aroma of eggs and onion might not prove irresistible to everyone. This makes great picnic fare. Pack it in a polybox, exclude the air, and transport it in a chiller bag with a selection of rolls and a bag of washed leaves.

Serves 4–6
8–10 eggs
6–8 spring onions (scallions)
    and/or I yellow or white onion,
    very finely chopped, plus extra
    to garnish
60–90ml/4–6 tbsp mayonnaise
mild French wholegrain mustard,
    to taste (optional)
15ml/1 tbsp chopped
    fresh parsley
salt and ground black pepper
rye toasts or crackers, to serve

Preparation: 3–4 minutes; Cooking: 12 minutes

1 Put the eggs in a large pan and pour in cold water to cover. Heat the water. When it boils, reduce the heat and simmer the eggs for 10 minutes. Stir the eggs twice so they cook evenly but don't let them become cracked or the contents will escape and cloud the water.

2 Drain the eggs, hold them under cold running water, then remove the shells, dry the eggs and chop roughly.

3 Place the chopped eggs in a large bowl. Add the onions, season with salt and pepper and mix well. Add enough mayonnaise to bind the mixture together.

4 Stir in the mustard, if using, and the chopped parsley, or sprinkle the parsley on top to garnish. If you have time, chill the mixture before serving with rye toasts or crackers.

Cook's Tip
Holding a freshly boiled egg under cold running water helps to prevent the yolk from acquiring a greenish tinge where it meets the white. Shell the eggs as soon as possible.

Spiced Feta with Chilli Seeds & Olives

What could be handier than jars of flavoured feta kept in the refrigerator? Chilli seeds flavour the marinated cubes of cheese spiked with spices and olives. Spoon the cheese cubes over green leaves and serve with warm bread as an appetizer.

Makes 4–5 small jars
500g/1¼ lb feta cheese
50g/2oz/½ cup stuffed olives
10ml/2 tsp coriander seeds
10ml/2 tsp whole peppercorns
5ml/1 tsp chilli seeds
few sprigs fresh rosemary or thyme
750ml/1¼ pints/3 cups virgin
    olive oil

Preparation: 15 minutes; Cooking: 0 minutes; Make ahead

1 Drain the feta cheese, discarding the liquid surrounding it, dice it and put it in a bowl. Slice the olives.

2 Using a pestle, crush the coriander seeds and peppercorns in a mortar and add them to the cheese with the olives, chilli seeds and rosemary or thyme leaves. Toss lightly.

3 Sterilize 4–5 small, clean glass jars by heating them in the oven at 150°C/300°F/Gas 2 for 15 minutes.

4 Spoon the cheese into the warm, dry sterilized jars and top up with olive oil, making sure that the cheese is well covered by the oil. Close the jars tightly and store them in the refrigerator for up to 3 weeks.

Cook's Tips
• The glass jars can also be sterilized by putting them through a hot wash in a dishwasher. As soon as the cycle is finished, while the jars are still warm, fill them with the cheese and oil. To ring the changes, use a garlic-infused oil, or try basil or chilli oil.
• Seal the jars with screw-topped or clip-down lids. The jars need to be totally airtight to keep the cheese fresh.

Chopped Eggs Energy 170kcal/706kJ; Protein 8.7g; Carbohydrate 0.5g, of which sugars 0.5g; Fat 15.1g, of which saturates 3.2g; Cholesterol 261mg; Calcium 48mg; Fibre 0.3g; Sodium 140mg.
Spiced Feta Energy 440kcal/1818kJ; Protein 15.7g; Carbohydrate 1.5g, of which sugars 1.5g; Fat 41.3g, of which saturates 16.7g; Cholesterol 70mg; Calcium 366mg; Fibre 0.3g; Sodium 1665mg.

Chilli Yogurt Cheese in Olive Oil

Yogurt, hung in muslin to drain off the whey, makes a superb soft cheese. Here it is bottled in olive oil with chilli and herbs, ready for serving on toast as a summer snack.

Fills 2 x 450g/1lb jars
800g/1¾lb/about 4 cups Greek (US strained, plain) yogurt
2.5ml/½ tsp salt
10ml/2 tsp crushed dried chillies or chilli powder
15ml/1 tbsp chopped fresh rosemary
15ml/1 tbsp chopped fresh thyme or oregano
about 300ml/½ pint/1¼ cups olive oil, preferably garlic-flavoured
lightly toasted country bread, to serve

Preparation: 2 minutes; Cooking: 18 minutes; Make ahead

1 Sterilize a 30cm/12in square of muslin (cheesecloth) by steeping it in boiling water. Drain and lay over a large plate. Mix the yogurt with the salt and tip on to the centre of the cloth. Bring up the sides of the cloth and tie firmly.

2 Hang the bag from a kitchen cabinet handle or in any convenient, cool position that allows a bowl to be placed underneath to catch the whey. Leave for 2–3 days until the yogurt stops dripping.

3 Sterilize two 450g/1lb clean glass preserving or jam jars by heating them in the oven at 150°C/300°F/Gas 2 for about 15 minutes or put them through a hot wash in a dishwasher.

4 Mix the dried chillies and herbs in a bowl. Take teaspoonfuls of the cheese and roll into balls between the palms of your hands. Lower into jars, sprinkling each layer with the herb and chilli mixture.

5 Pour the oil over the cheese until the balls are completely covered. Close the jars tightly and store in the refrigerator for up to 3 weeks. To serve the cheese, spoon out of the jars with a little of the flavoured olive oil and spread on to fresh or lightly toasted farmhouse bread.

Vegetarian Chopped Liver

This mixture of browned onions, chopped vegetables, hard-boiled egg and walnuts looks and tastes surprisingly like chopped liver but is lighter and fresher.

Serves 6
90ml/6 tbsp vegetable oil, plus extra if necessary
3 onions, chopped
175–200g/6–7oz/1½–scant 1¾ cups frozen peas
115–150g/4–5oz/1 cup green beans, roughly chopped
15 walnuts, shelled (30 halves)
3 eggs
salt and ground black pepper
slices of rye bread or crisp matzos, to serve

Preparation: 7–8 minutes; Cooking: 10 minutes

1 Boil the eggs in a pan of water for 10 minutes. Drain, plunge into cold water and leave until cold, then shell.

2 Meanwhile, heat the oil in a pan, add the onions and fry until softened and lightly browned. Add the peas and beans and season with salt and pepper to taste. Continue to cook until the vegetables are tender and the beans are no longer bright green but look fairly pale.

3 Put the vegetables in a food processor, add the walnuts and eggs and process until the mixture forms a thick paste. Taste for seasoning and, if the mixture seems a bit dry, add a little more oil and mix in thoroughly. Serve the nutty vegetable mixture with slices of rye bread or matzos.

Cook's Tips
If you are serving this to vegetarians, you might want to change the name, since even mentioning the words 'chopped liver' could put them off. This would be a shame, as the dish is really tasty and nutritious. The walnuts add fibre and flavour, with the added bonus that they are a good source of omega-3 fatty acids, which help to keep the heart healthy. Walnuts are also a valuable source of potassium, magnesium, iron, zinc, copper and selenium.

Chilli Yogurt Energy 1331kcal/5488kJ; Protein 24g; Carbohydrate 7.5g, of which sugars 7.5g; Fat 138.2g, of which saturates 33.8g; Cholesterol 0mg; Calcium 563mg; Fibre 0g; Sodium 758mg.
Chopped Liver Energy 309kcal/1277kJ; Protein 9g; Carbohydrate 11.1g, of which sugars 6.2g; Fat 25.9g, of which saturates 3.4g; Cholesterol 95mg; Calcium 64mg; Fibre 3.6g; Sodium 39mg.

Pears with Blue Cheese & Walnuts

Succulent pears filled with blue cheese and walnut cream look pretty on colourful leaves and make a great appetizer.

Serves 6
115g/4oz fresh cream cheese
75g/3oz Stilton or other mature
  blue cheese, such as Roquefort
30–45ml/2–3 tbsp single
  (light) cream
115g/4oz/1 cup roughly
  chopped walnuts

6 ripe pears
15ml/1 tbsp lemon juice
mixed salad leaves, such as frisée,
  oakleaf lettuce and radicchio
6 cherry tomatoes
sea salt and ground black pepper
walnut halves and sprigs of fresh
  flat leaf parsley, to garnish

For the dressing
juice of 1 lemon
a little finely grated lemon rind
a pinch of caster (superfine) sugar
60ml/4 tbsp olive oil

Preparation: 8–10 minutes; Cooking: 0 minutes

1 Mash the cream cheese and blue cheese together in a mixing bowl with a good grinding of black pepper, then blend in the cream to make a smooth mixture. Add 25g/1oz/¼ cup of the chopped walnuts and mix to distribute evenly.

2 Peel and halve the pears and scoop out the core from each. Put the pears into a bowl of water with the 15ml/1 tbsp lemon juice to prevent them from browning. Make the dressing by whisking the ingredients together in a small bowl, and then add salt and pepper to taste.

3 Arrange a bed of salad leaves on six plates – shallow soup plates are ideal – add a cherry tomato to each and sprinkle over the remaining chopped walnuts.

4 Drain the pears well and pat dry with kitchen paper, then turn them in the prepared dressing and arrange, hollow side up, on the salad leaves.

5 Divide the blue cheese filling among the 12 pear halves and spoon the dressing over the top. Garnish each filled pear half with a walnut half and a sprig of flat leaf parsley before serving.

White Beans in a Spicy Dressing

Tender white beans are delicious in this spicy sauce with the bite of fresh, crunchy green pepper and the flavour of juicy tomatoes. It is perfect for preparing ahead of time.

Serves 4
750g/1⅔lb tomatoes, diced
1 onion, finely chopped
½–1 mild fresh chilli, finely
  chopped

1 green (bell) pepper, seeded
  and chopped
pinch of sugar
4 garlic cloves, chopped
400g/14oz can cannellini
  beans, drained
45–60ml/3–4 tbsp olive oil
grated rind and juice of 1 lemon
15ml/1 tbsp cider vinegar or
  wine vinegar
salt and ground black pepper
chopped fresh parsley or
  coriander (cilantro), to garnish

Preparation: 7 minutes; Cooking: 0 minutes; Chilling: 2–3 hours

1 Put the tomatoes, onion, chilli, green pepper, sugar, garlic, cannellini beans, salt and plenty of ground black pepper in a large bowl and toss together until well combined.

2 Add the olive oil, grated lemon rind, lemon juice and vinegar to the salad and toss lightly to combine.

3 Cover and chill for 2–3 hours if time permits. Garnish the bean salad with chopped parsley or coriander and serve with toasted pitta breads.

Variations
• Substitute flageolets (small cannellini), or try using haricots (navy beans). They will all taste and look attractive.
• Instead of serving the salad with toasted pitta bread, it could be used as a filling for pitta pockets. Warm 4 large pitta breads under a medium grill (broiler). Alternatively, place them between sheets of kitchen paper and warm them in a microwave on High for 1–2 minutes. Cut the breads in half through the middle and open each half up to make 8 pitta pockets. Spoon the salad into each pitta pocket.

Pears Energy 322kcal/1332kJ; Protein 5.1g; Carbohydrate 15.7g, of which sugars 15.7g; Fat 26.9g, of which saturates 10.2g; Cholesterol 30mg; Calcium 109mg; Fibre 3.7g; Sodium 218mg.
White Beans Energy 391kcal/1654kJ; Protein 24g; Carbohydrate 53.8g, of which sugars 11.8g; Fat 10.4g, of which saturates 1.6g; Cholesterol 0mg; Calcium 120mg; Fibre 18.5g; Sodium 37mg.

Deep-fried Onion Rings

These are a very popular side dish, which provide a crisp contrast when served with sliced hard-boiled eggs or fried mushrooms.

Serves 4
2 Spanish onions, thickly sliced
1 large egg white, lightly beaten
60ml/4 tbsp plain
  (all-purpose) flour
groundnut oil for deep-frying
salt and ground black pepper

Preparation: 4 minutes; Cooking: 6 minutes

1 Separate the onion slices into rings. Dip them into the egg white and stir to coat on all sides.

2 Season the flour with salt and pepper, then dip the onion rings into it, one at a time, until evenly coated.

3 Heat the oil for deep-frying to 190°C/375°F, or until a cube of day-old bread browns in 30–40 seconds. Fry the onion rings for 3–4 minutes, until browned and crisp. Drain on kitchen paper and serve immediately.

Variations
• *For corn-crusted onion rings, soak red onion rings in milk for about 30 minutes. Drain, then dip into coarse cornmeal (polenta), mixed with a pinch each of dried red chilli flakes, paprika and ground toasted cumin seeds. Deep-fry.*
• *For spicy onion rings, mix 90ml/6 tbsp chick-pea flour (besan or gram flour) with 2.5ml/½ tsp each of ground cumin, ground coriander, chilli powder and garam masala. Season and add 1 chopped green chilli and 30ml/2 tbsp chopped fresh coriander (cilantro). Mix with 45–60ml/3–4 tbsp cold water to make a fairly thick batter. Dip the onion rings into the batter, then deep-fry until crisp.*
• *For onion tempura, beat 2 egg yolks with 150ml/¼ pint/⅔ cup iced sparkling water. Lightly mix in 115g/4oz sifted self-raising (self-rising) flour and a pinch of salt, leaving the batter lumpy. Dip onion rings into the batter and deep-fry.*

Rice Tortitas

Like miniature tortillas, these little rice pancakes are good served hot, either plain or with tomato sauce for dipping. They make an excellent scoop for any soft vegetable mixture or dip – a very Spanish way of eating.

Serves 4
30ml/2 tbsp olive oil
115g/4oz/1 cup cooked long grain white rice
1 potato, grated
4 spring onions (scallions), thinly sliced
1 garlic clove, finely chopped
15ml/1 tbsp chopped fresh parsley
3 large (US extra large) eggs, beaten
2.5ml/½ tsp paprika
salt and ground black pepper

Preparation: 6–7 minutes; Cooking: 11–12 minutes

1 Heat half the olive oil in a large frying pan and stir-fry the rice, with the potato, spring onions and garlic, over a high heat for 3 minutes until golden.

2 Tip the rice and vegetable mixture into a bowl and stir in the parsley and eggs, with the paprika and plenty of salt and pepper. Mix well.

3 Heat the remaining oil in the frying pan and drop in large spoonfuls of the rice mixture, leaving room for spreading. Cook the tortitas for 1–2 minutes on each side.

4 Drain the tortitas on kitchen paper and keep hot while cooking the remaining mixture. Pile the cooked tortitas on a serving platter or on individual plates and serve hot.

Cook's Tip
These tortitas can be used as a base, for example for cooked chicken livers, instead of the usual sliced bread. Children like them as they are, with a puddle of tomato ketchup for dipping.

Onion Rings Energy 214kcal/880kJ; Protein 1.4g; Carbohydrate 8.9g, of which sugars 6.3g; Fat 19.5g, of which saturates 2.3g; Cholesterol 0mg; Calcium 28mg; Fibre 1.6g; Sodium 4mg.
Rice Tortitas Energy 185kcal/776kJ; Protein 6.8g; Carbohydrate 17.6g, of which sugars 1.2g; Fat 10.4g, of which saturates 2.1g; Cholesterol 143mg; Calcium 56mg; Fibre 1.3g; Sodium 63mg.

Toasted Ciabatta with Tomatoes, Cheese & Marjoram Flowers

Here is a very simple but tasty method of using marjoram flowers. The combination of cheese, tomato and marjoram is popular, but lots of extras can be added, such as capers, olives or slices of roasted peppers.

Serves 2
1 ciabatta loaf
4 tomatoes
115g/4oz mozzarella or
    Cheddar cheese
15ml/1 tbsp olive oil
15ml/1 tbsp marjoram flowers
salt and ground black pepper

Preparation: 4 minutes; Cooking: 4–5 minutes

1 Preheat the grill (broiler) to high. Cut the loaf in half lengthwise and toast very lightly under the grill until it has turned a pale golden brown.

2 Meanwhile, skin the tomatoes by plunging them in boiling water for 30 seconds, then refreshing them in cold water. Peel and cut into thick slices.

3 Slice or grate the mozzarella or Cheddar cheese. Lightly drizzle the olive oil over the bread and top with the tomato slices and sliced or grated cheese. Season with salt and pepper and scatter the marjoram flowers over the top. Drizzle with a little more olive oil.

4 Place under the hot grill until the cheese bubbles and is just starting to brown. Serve immediately.

Cook's Tip
Add marjoram flowers to your favourite pizza topping. Sprinkle over 7.5–15ml/½–1 tbsp flowers or flowering tops and add a few of the leaves. The flavours are strong, so marjoram flowers should be used with care, especially if you haven't tried them before. The amount you use will depend on your own palate.

Tomato & Mozzarella Toasts

These resemble mini pizzas and are good with drinks before a dinner party. You can prepare them several hours in advance and pop them in the oven just as your guests arrive. Ring the changes as regards toppings to satisfy meat-eaters and vegetarians alike.

Serves 6–8
3 sfilatini (thin ciabatta)
about 250ml/8 fl oz/1 cup
    sun-dried tomato purée (paste)
3 x 150g/5oz packets mozzarella
    cheese, drained and chopped
about 10ml/2 tsp dried oregano
    or mixed herbs
30–45ml/2–3 tbsp olive oil
ground black pepper

Preparation: 3 minutes; Cooking: 7 minutes

1 Preheat the oven to 220°C/425°F/Gas 7. Also preheat the grill (broiler). Cut each sfilatino on the diagonal into 12–15 slices, discarding the ends.

2 Grill (broil) until lightly toasted on both sides. Spread sun-dried tomato purée on one side of each slice of toast. Arrange the mozzarella over the tomato purée.

3 Put the toasts on baking sheets, sprinkle with herbs and pepper to taste and drizzle with oil. Bake for 5 minutes, or until the mozzarella has melted and is bubbling. Leave the toasts to settle for a few minutes before serving.

Variations
These tasty toast treats are capable of infinite variation. Instead of sun-dried tomato purée or paste, try spreading them with a fruity chutney, a mild piquant pepper ketchup or even Dijon mustard. Extra toppings could include olives or figs.

Cook's Tip
Mozzarella can also be bought as tiny balls. If you prefer to use these, just halve them and place on top of the tomato purée.

Ciabatta Energy 502kcal/2113kJ; Protein 22.3g; Carbohydrate 58.2g, of which sugars 9.3g; Fat 21.7g, of which saturates 9.5g; Cholesterol 33mg; Calcium 343mg; Fibre 4.3g; Sodium 783mg.
Toasts Energy 227kcal/947kJ; Protein 13.3g; Carbohydrate 10.9g, of which sugars 4.8g; Fat 14.8g, of which saturates 8.2g; Cholesterol 33mg; Calcium 230mg; Fibre 1.2g; Sodium 365mg.

Spiced Plantain Chips

Plantains are more starchy than the bananas to which they are related, and must be cooked before being eaten. In Latin America the fruit is used much as a potato would be. This snack has a lovely sweet taste, which is balanced by the heat from the chilli powder and sauce. Cook the chips just before you plan to serve them.

Serves 4
2 large plantains
oil, for shallow frying
2.5ml/½ tsp chilli powder
5ml/1 tsp ground cinnamon
hot chilli sauce, to serve

Preparation: 2 minutes; Cooking: 6 minutes

1 Peel the plaintains. Cut off and throw away the ends, then slice the fruit into rounds, cutting slightly on the diagonal to give larger, flatter slices.

2 Pour the oil for frying into a small frying pan, to a depth of about 1cm/½in. Heat the oil until it is very hot, watching it closely all the time. It should register 190°C/375°F on a sugar thermometer. Test by carefully adding a slice of plantain; it should float and the oil should immediately bubble up around it.

3 Fry the plantain slices in small batches or the temperature of the oil will drop. When they are golden brown remove from the oil with a slotted spoon and drain on kitchen paper. Keep hot while cooking successive batches.

4 Mix the chilli powder with the cinnamon. Put the plantain chips on a serving plate, sprinkle them with the chilli and cinnamon mixture and serve immediately, with a small bowl of hot chilli sauce for dipping.

> **Cook's Tip**
> Plantain skins are very dark, almost black, when the fruit is ready to eat. If they are green when you buy them, allow them to ripen at room temperature for a few days before use.

Mozzarella in Carozza with Fresh Tomato Salsa

The title of this delectable Italian snack translates as cheese 'in a carriage'. The recipe is similar to croque monsieur, except that it contains mozzarella and is dipped in egg and fried.

Serves 4
200g/7oz mozzarella cheese, thinly sliced
8 thin slices of bread, crusts removed
a little dried oregano
30ml/2 tbsp freshly grated strong hard cheese
3 eggs, beaten
olive oil, for frying
salt and ground black pepper
fresh herbs, to garnish

For the salsa
4 ripe plum tomatoes, peeled, seeded and finely chopped
15ml/1 tbsp chopped fresh parsley
5ml/1 tsp balsamic vinegar
15ml/1 tbsp extra virgin olive oil

Preparation: 7 minutes; Cooking: 8 minutes; Standing: 5–10 minutes

1 Arrange the mozzarella on four slices of the bread. Season with salt and pepper and sprinkle with a little dried oregano and the grated cheese. Top with the other bread slices and press them firmly together.

2 Pour the beaten eggs into a large shallow dish and season with salt and pepper. Add the cheese sandwiches, two at a time, pressing them into the egg with a fish slice or metal spatula until they are well coated. Repeat with the remaining sandwiches, then leave them to stand for 5–10 minutes.

3 To make the salsa, put the chopped tomatoes in a bowl and add the parsley. Stir in the vinegar and the extra virgin olive oil. Season well with salt and pepper and set aside.

4 Heat olive oil to a depth of 5mm/¼in in a large frying pan. Carefully add the sandwiches in batches and cook for about 2 minutes on each side until golden and crisp. Drain well on kitchen paper. Cut in half and serve garnished with fresh herbs and accompanied by the salsa.

Plantain Chips Energy 193kcal/806kJ; Protein 1.1g; Carbohydrate 22.7g, of which sugars 4.3g; Fat 11.5g, of which saturates 1.4g; Cholesterol 0mg; Calcium 23mg; Fibre 1.6g; Sodium 14mg.
Mozzarella Energy 472kcal/1968kJ; Protein 21.7g; Carbohydrate 27g, of which sugars 3.6g; Fat 31.7g, of which saturates 11.6g; Cholesterol 179mg; Calcium 353mg; Fibre 1.5g; Sodium 599mg.

Corn Fritters

Sometimes it is the simplest dishes that taste the best. These tasty fritters, packed with corn, are easy to prepare and go well with everything from gammon to nut rissoles.

Makes 12
3 corn cobs, total weight about 250g/9oz
1 garlic clove, crushed
a small bunch of fresh coriander (cilantro), chopped
1 small fresh red or green chilli, seeded and finely chopped
1 spring onion (scallion), finely chopped
15ml/1 tbsp soy sauce
75g/3oz/³/₄ cup rice flour or plain (all-purpose) flour
2 eggs, lightly beaten
60ml/4 tbsp water
oil, for shallow-frying
salt and ground black pepper
sweet chilli sauce or tomato ketchup, to serve

Preparation: 5 minutes; Cooking: 8 minutes

1 Using a sharp knife, slice the kernels from the cobs using downward strokes. Rinse to remove any clinging debris from the cob. Place all the kernels in a bowl.

2 Add the garlic, chopped coriander, red or green chilli, spring onion, soy sauce, flour, beaten eggs and water to the corn and mix well. Season with salt and pepper to taste and mix again. The mixture should be firm enough to hold its shape, but not so stiff that it is unworkable.

3 Heat the oil in a large frying pan. Add spoonfuls of the corn mixture, gently spreading each one out with the back of the spoon to make a roundish fritter. Cook for 1–2 minutes on each side, turning carefully with a spatula.

4 Drain the first batch of fritters on kitchen paper and keep hot on a foil-covered dish while frying more. Serve the fritters hot with sweet chilli sauce or tomato ketchup – arrange on a large plate around the sauce, if you like. Alternatively, serve the fritters on individual plates, giving each guest their own bowl of dipping sauce. An egg cup makes a novel container for this, or use one of the miniature Chinese bowls intended for soy sauce.

Cheese Aigrettes

These choux buns, flavoured with mature Gruyère and dusted with extra cheese, are a bit fiddly to make, but the dough can be prepared ahead and then deep fried.

Makes 30
100g/3³/₄oz/scant 1 cup strong plain (all-purpose) flour
2.5ml/¹/₂ tsp paprika
2.5ml/¹/₂ tsp salt
75g/3oz/6 tbsp cold butter, diced
200ml/7fl oz/scant 1 cup water
3 eggs, beaten
75g/3oz/³/₄ cup coarsely grated mature Gruyère cheese
corn or vegetable oil, for deep frying
50g/2oz piece of strong hard cheese, finely grated
ground black pepper
sprigs of flat leaf parsley, to garnish

Preparation: 8 minutes; Cooking: 9–12 minutes

1 Sift the flour, paprika and salt on to a large sheet of foil or baking parchment. Add a generous grinding of black pepper.

2 Put the butter and water into a medium pan and heat gently. As soon as the butter has melted and the liquid starts to boil, tip in all the seasoned flour at once and beat hard with a wooden spoon until the dough forms a ball and comes away from the sides of the pan.

3 Remove the pan from the heat and cool the paste for 5 minutes. This step is important if the aigrettes are to rise well. Gradually beat in enough of the beaten egg to give a stiff dropping consistency that still holds a shape on the spoon. Mix in the Gruyère.

4 Heat the oil for deep frying to 180°C/350°F or until a cube of bread, added to the hot oil, browns in about 1 minute. Take a teaspoonful of the choux paste and use a second spoon to slide it into the oil. Make more aigrettes in the same way. Fry for 3–4 minutes until golden brown. Drain on kitchen paper and keep warm while cooking successive batches.

5 To serve, pile the aigrettes on a warmed serving dish, sprinkle with cheese and garnish with sprigs of parsley.

Cheese Aigrettes Energy 84kcal/348kJ; Protein 2.2g; Carbohydrate 2.4g, of which sugars 0.1g; Fat 7.3g, of which saturates 2.7g; Cholesterol 28mg; Calcium 46mg; Fibre 0.1g; Sodium 58mg.
Corn Fritters Energy 76kcal/314kJ; Protein 2.1g; Carbohydrate 7.6g, of which sugars 0.5g; Fat 4.1g, of which saturates 0.7g; Cholesterol 32mg; Calcium 14mg; Fibre 0.6g; Sodium 102mg.

Courgette Rissoles

This is an ingenious way of transforming bland-tasting courgettes into a dish that captivates everyone who tries it.

Serves 3–4
500g/1¼lb courgettes (zucchini)
120ml/4fl oz/½ cup extra virgin olive oil
1 large onion, finely chopped
2 spring onions (scallions), green and white parts finely chopped
1 garlic clove, crushed
3 medium slices proper bread (not from a pre-sliced loaf)
2 eggs, lightly beaten
200g/7oz feta cheese, crumbled
50g/2oz/½ cup freshly grated Greek Graviera or strong hard cheese
45–60ml/3–4 tbsp finely chopped fresh dill or 5ml/1 tsp dried oregano
50g/2oz/½ cup plain (all-purpose) flour
salt and ground black pepper
lemon wedges, to serve

Preparation: 5–6 minutes; Cooking: 14 minutes

1 Slice the courgettes into 4cm/1½in lengths and cook in a pan of boiling salted water for 10 minutes, until very soft. Drain in a colander and set aside until cool enough to handle.

2 Heat 45ml/3 tbsp of the oil in a frying pan and sauté the onion and spring onions until transparent. Add the garlic, cook for 1 minute, then remove from the heat and set aside.

3 Squeeze the courgettes to remove as much liquid as possible, then tip into a large bowl. Stir in the onion mixture and mix well.

4 Toast the bread, remove the crusts and crumb it in a food processor. Add to the courgette and onion mixture, then stir in the eggs, feta and grated cheese.

5 Stir in the herbs, with salt and pepper to taste. Mix well, adding a little flour if needed. Shape the mixture into 6–8 rissoles and coat them lightly in flour.

6 Heat the remaining oil in a large frying pan and fry the rissoles until crisp and brown all over. Drain on kitchen paper and serve hot, with lemon wedges for squeezing.

Golden Gruyère & Basil Tortillas

Tortilla flip-overs are a great invention. Once you've tried this recipe, you'll want to experiment with lots of different fillings, and leftovers will never go to waste again.

Serves 2
15ml/1 tbsp olive oil
2 soft flour tortillas
115g/4oz Gruyère cheese, thinly sliced
a handful of fresh basil leaves
salt and ground black pepper

Preparation: 1–2 minutes; Cooking: 4 minutes

1 Heat the oil in a frying pan over a medium heat. Add one of the tortillas, and heat through for 1 minute.

2 Arrange the Gruyère cheese slices and basil leaves on top of the tortilla and season with salt and pepper.

3 Place the remaining tortilla on top to make a sandwich and flip the whole thing over with a metal spatula. Cook for a few minutes, until the underneath is golden.

4 Slide the tortilla sandwich on to a chopping board or plate and cut into wedges. Serve immediately.

Variations
• Try adding some onion to the tortilla for a tasty alternative: cook onion rings in water until tender, then drain and sandwich with the cheese.
• You could also add some sliced fresh tomato to the tortilla, if you like. Or even some sun-dried tomatoes for a more intense flavour.
• If you've been cooking pasta and have made too much sauce, this recipe is a perfect way of using the surplus. Simply spread a little on to the cheese before adding the top tortilla.
• Instead of Gruyère, you could use Pecorino Romano or another strong hard cheese.
• Spice up your tortilla with some chopped chillies, if you like. Try different varieties for different heats.

Rissoles Energy 528kcal/2194kJ; Protein 22g; Carbohydrate 28.8g, of which sugars 7.9g; Fat 36.9g, of which saturates 13g; Cholesterol 143mg; Calcium 436mg; Fibre 3g; Sodium 1001mg.
Tortillas Energy 354kcal/1474kJ; Protein 16.4g; Carbohydrate 15g, of which sugars 0.4g; Fat 24.6g, of which saturates 13.3g; Cholesterol 56mg; Calcium 453mg; Fibre 0.6g; Sodium 486mg.

Samosas

Throughout the East, they are sold by street vendors, and eaten at any time of day.

Makes about 20
1 packet 25cm/10in square
   spring roll wrappers, thawed
   if frozen
30ml/2 tbsp plain (all-purpose)
   flour, mixed to a paste
   with water
vegetable oil, for deep frying
coriander (cilantro) leaves,
   to garnish

For the filling
25g/1oz/2 tbsp ghee or
   unsalted butter

1 small onion, finely chopped
1cm/½ in piece fresh root ginger,
   peeled and chopped
1 garlic glove, crushed
2.5ml/½ tsp chilli powder
1 large potato, about 225g/8oz,
   cooked until just tender and
   finely diced
50g/2oz/½ cup cauliflower
   florets, lightly cooked, chopped
   into small pieces
50g/2oz/½ cup frozen
   peas, thawed
5–10ml/1–2 tsp garam masala
15ml/1 tbsp chopped fresh
   coriander (leaves and stems)
squeeze of lemon juice
salt

Preparation: 8 minutes; Cooking: 12 minutes

1 Heat the ghee or butter in a large frying pan and fry the onion, ginger and garlic for 5 minutes until the onion has softened but not browned. Add the chilli powder and cook for 1 minute, then stir in the potato, cauliflower and peas. Sprinkle with garam masala and set aside to cool. Stir in the chopped coriander, lemon juice and salt.

2 Cut the spring roll wrappers into three strips (or two for larger samosas). Brush the edges with a little of the flour paste. Place a small spoonful of filling about 2cm/¾in in from the edge of one strip. Fold one corner over the filling to make a triangle and continue this folding until the entire strip has been used and a triangular pastry has been formed. Seal any open edges with more flour and water paste.

3 Heat the oil for deep frying to 190°C/375°F and fry the samosas, a few at a time, until golden and crisp. Drain well on kitchen paper and serve hot garnished with coriander leaves.

Molettes

This is the Mexican version of beans on toast. Sold by street traders around mid-morning, they make the perfect snack for those who have missed breakfast. A nourishing and sustaining snack, it would taste good at any time.

Serves 4
4 crusty finger rolls
50g/2oz/¼ cup butter, softened
225g/8oz/1⅓ cups refried beans
150g/5oz/1¼ cups grated
   medium Cheddar cheese
green salad leaves, to garnish
120ml/4fl oz/½ cup classic
   tomato salsa, to serve

Preparation: 2 minutes; Cooking: 7 minutes

1 Cut the rolls in half, then take a sliver off the base so that they lie flat. Remove a little of the crumbs. Spread them lightly with enough butter to cover.

2 Arrange them on a baking sheet and grill (broil) for about 5 minutes, or until they are crisp and golden. Meanwhile, heat the refried beans over a low heat in a small pan.

3 Scoop the beans into the rolls, then sprinkle the grated cheese on top. Pop back under the grill until the cheese melts. Serve with the tomato salsa and garnish with salad leaves.

> **Cook's Tips**
> • Refried beans can be made at home, but the process is quite a lengthy one – not really suitable for a book that aims to save you time. Fortunately the product now comes in cans, so look out for them in the Mexican aisle at the supermarket.
> • To make the salsa, roast 3 Serrano chillies over the flame of a gas burner until they char. Place them in a plastic bag for 20 minutes so that the steam softens them, then skin them, remove the seeds and chop the flesh. Chop 1 onion and soak it in the juice of 2 limes. Peel and dice 8 firm but ripe tomatoes. Chop a large bunch of fresh coriander (cilantro). Mix all these ingredients in a bowl and add a generous pinch each of sugar and salt. Chill before serving if possible.

Molettes Energy 450kcal/1886kJ; Protein 19.2g; Carbohydrate 39.9g, of which sugars 4.2g; Fat 24.1g, of which saturates 15g; Cholesterol 63mg; Calcium 392mg; Fibre 4.5g; Sodium 889mg.
Samosas Energy 56kcal/235kJ; Protein 1.3g; Carbohydrate 10g, of which sugars 0.8g; Fat 1.4g, of which saturates 0.2g; Cholesterol 0mg; Calcium 16mg; Fibre 0.7g; Sodium 8mg.

Soufflé Omelette with Mushrooms

A soufflé omelette makes an ideal meal for one, especially with this delicious filling, but be warned – when others smell it cooking they are likely to demand their share.

Serves 1
2 eggs, separated
15g/½oz/1 tbsp butter
flat leaf parsley or coriander
   (cilantro) leaves, to garnish

For the mushroom sauce
15g/½oz/1 tbsp butter
75g/3oz/generous 1 cup button
   (white) mushrooms,
   thinly sliced
15ml/1 tbsp plain
   (all-purpose) flour
85–120ml/3–4fl oz/⅓–½ cup
   semi-skimmed (low-fat) milk
5ml/1 tsp chopped fresh parsley
salt and ground black pepper

Preparation: 5 minutes; Cooking: 13–15 minutes

1 To make the mushroom sauce, melt the butter in a pan or frying pan and add the sliced mushrooms. Fry gently for 4–5 minutes, stirring occasionally. The mushrooms will exude quite a lot of liquid, but this will rapidly be reabsorbed.

2 Stir in the flour, then gradually add the milk, stirring all the time. Cook until the sauce boils and thickens. Add the parsley, if using, and season with salt and pepper. Keep warm.

3 Make the omelette. Beat the egg yolks with 15ml/1 tbsp water and season with a little salt and pepper. Whisk the egg whites until stiff, then fold into the egg yolks. Preheat the grill (broiler) for at least 3 minutes.

4 Meanwhile, melt the butter in a large frying pan. Pour in the egg mixture. Cook over a gentle heat for 2–4 minutes.

5 Place the frying pan under the grill and cook for a further 3–4 minutes until the top of the omelette has puffed up and has turned a golden brown colour.

6 Slide the omelette on to a warmed serving plate, pour the mushroom sauce over the top and fold the omelette in half. Serve, garnished with parsley.

Mexican Tortilla Parcels

Seeded green chillies add just a flicker of fire to the spicy tomato filling in these parcels, which are perfect as a main course or snack.

Serves 4
675g/1½lb tomatoes
60ml/4 tbsp sunflower oil
1 large onion, finely sliced
1 garlic clove, crushed
10ml/2 tsp cumin seeds
2 fresh green chillies, seeded
   and chopped
30ml/2 tbsp tomato purée
   (paste)
1 vegetable stock (bouillon) cube
200g/7oz can corn, drained
15ml/1 tbsp chopped fresh
   coriander (cilantro)
115g/4oz/1 cup grated
   Cheddar cheese
8 wheat tortillas
fresh coriander (cilantro),
   shredded lettuce and sour
   cream, to serve

Preparation: 5 minutes; Cooking: 14 minutes

1 Peel the tomatoes: place them in a heatproof bowl, add boiling water to cover and leave for 30 seconds. Lift out with a slotted spoon and plunge into a bowl of cold water. Leave for 1 minute, then drain. Slip the skins off the tomatoes and chop.

2 Heat half the oil in a frying pan and fry the onion with the garlic and cumin seeds for 5 minutes, until the onion softens. Add the chillies and tomatoes, then stir in the tomato purée. Crumble the stock cube over, stir well and cook gently for 5 minutes, until the chilli is soft but the tomato has not completely broken down. Stir in the corn and fresh coriander and heat gently to warm through. Keep warm.

3 Sprinkle grated cheese in the middle of each tortilla. Spoon some tomato mixture over the cheese. Fold over one edge of the tortilla, then the sides and finally the remaining edge, to enclose the filling completely.

4 Heat the remaining oil in a frying pan and fry the filled tortillas for 1–2 minutes on each side until golden and crisp. Lift them out carefully with tongs and drain on kitchen paper. Serve immediately, with coriander, shredded lettuce and sour cream.

Soufflé Omelette Energy 838kcal/3514kJ; Protein 45.5g; Carbohydrate 53.7g, of which sugars 42.1g; Fat 51.4g, of which saturates 28.3g; Cholesterol 497mg; Calcium 1150mg; Fibre 1.3g; Sodium 707mg.
Tortilla Parcels Energy 576kcal/2424kJ; Protein 17.5g; Carbohydrate 79.3g, of which sugars 12.2g; Fat 22.5g, of which saturates 7.8g; Cholesterol 28mg; Calcium 339mg; Fibre 5g; Sodium 656mg.

Vegetable & Egg Noodle Ribbons

Serve this elegant, colourful dish with a tossed green salad as a light lunch. Use fresh pasta noodles for optimum speed and maximum flavour.

Serves 4
1 large carrot, peeled
2 courgettes (zucchini)
50g/2oz/¼ cup butter
15ml/1 tbsp olive oil
6 fresh shiitake mushrooms, finely sliced
50g/2oz/½ cup frozen peas, thawed
350g/12oz fresh broad egg ribbon noodles
10ml/2 tsp chopped fresh mixed herbs, such as marjoram, chives and basil
salt and ground black pepper
25g/1oz strong hard cheese, to serve (optional)

Preparation: 3 minutes; Cooking: 7 minutes

1 Using a vegetable peeler, carefully slice thin strips from the carrot and the courgettes.

2 Heat the butter with the olive oil in a large frying pan. Stir in the carrots and shiitake mushrooms; fry for 2 minutes. Add the courgettes and peas and stir-fry until the courgettes are cooked, but still crisp. Season with salt and pepper.

3 Meanwhile, cook the noodles in a large pan of boiling water until just tender. Drain the noodles well and tip them into a bowl. Add the vegetables and toss gently to mix.

4 Sprinkle over the fresh herbs and season to taste. If using the cheese, grate or shave it over the top. Toss lightly and serve in the large bowl or in individual pasta bowls.

Variation
When fresh young green peas are in season, use them instead of the frozen peas. Their flavour is incomparable and they need very little cooking. To obtain 50g/2oz podded peas you will need to buy at least double that weight in pods. Mangetouts (snow peas) would also taste good in this noodle dish.

Sesame-tossed Asparagus with Noodles

Tender asparagus spears tossed with sesame seeds and served on a bed of crispy, deep-fried noodles makes a lovely dish for casual entertaining.

Serves 4
15ml/1 tbsp sunflower oil
350g/12oz thin asparagus spears, trimmed
5ml/1 tsp salt
5ml/1 tsp ground black pepper
5ml/1 tsp golden caster (superfine) sugar
30ml/2 tbsp Chinese cooking wine or sherry
45ml/3 tbsp light soy sauce
60ml/4 tbsp vegetarian oyster sauce
10ml/2 tsp sesame oil
60ml/4 tbsp toasted sesame seeds

For the noodles
50g/2oz dried bean thread noodles or thin rice noodles
sunflower oil, for frying

Preparation: 2–3 minutes; Cooking: 7–8 minutes

1 First make the crispy noodles. Fill a wok one-third full of oil and heat to 180°C/350°F (or until a cube of bread, dropped into the oil, browns in 15 seconds). Add the noodles, small bunches at a time, to the oil; they will crisp and puff up in seconds. Using a slotted spoon, remove from the wok and drain on kitchen paper. Set aside.

2 Heat a clean wok over a high heat and add the sunflower oil. Add the asparagus and stir-fry for 3 minutes.

3 Put four bowls to warm so that they are ready for serving.

4 Add the salt, pepper, sugar and wine or sherry to the wok with the soy sauce and oyster sauce. Stir-fry for 2–3 minutes. Add the sesame oil, toss and remove from the heat.

5 To serve, divide the crispy noodles between four warmed plates or bowls and top with the asparagus and juices. Sprinkle over the toasted sesame seeds and serve immediately.

Vegetable Ribbons Energy 500kcal/2100kJ; Protein 13.9g; Carbohydrate 68.1g, of which sugars 5.6g; Fat 21g, of which saturates 9.1g; Cholesterol 53mg; Calcium 62mg; Fibre 4.9g; Sodium 242mg.
Asparagus with Noodles Energy 131kcal/547kJ; Protein 4.6g; Carbohydrate 16.5g, of which sugars 6.9g; Fat 5.6g, of which saturates 0.6g; Cholesterol 0mg; Calcium 31mg; Fibre 2g; Sodium 1047mg.

Spaghetti with Garlic & Oil

It doesn't get much simpler than this: spaghetti tossed with the very best olive oil, with chilli for a hint of heat and plenty of parsley for a contrasting cool, fresh flavour. If you use fresh pasta, this is one of the quickest dishes there is.

Serves 4
400g/14oz fresh or dried
  spaghetti
90ml/6 tbsp extra virgin olive oil
2–4 garlic cloves, crushed
1 dried red chilli
1 small handful fresh flat leaf
  parsley, roughly chopped
salt

Preparation: 1 minute; Cooking: 4–12 minutes

1 Cook the pasta in a large pan of lightly salted boiling water. Dried pasta will take 10–12 minutes, fresh about 3 minutes. Fresh pasta is ready when it rises to the surface of the water.

2 Meanwhile, heat the oil very gently in a small frying pan. Add the crushed garlic and whole dried chilli and stir over a low heat until the garlic is just beginning to brown. Remove the chilli, which is only used to flavour the oil, and discard.

3 Drain the pasta and tip it into a warmed large bowl. Pour on the oil and garlic mixture, add the parsley and toss vigorously until the pasta glistens. Serve immediately, either in the bowl used for mixing or in individual warmed bowls.

Cook's Tips
• *Since the oil is such an important ingredient here, only use the very best cold-pressed extra virgin olive oil.*
• *Don't use salt in the oil and garlic mixture, because it will not dissolve sufficiently. This is why salt is recommended for cooking the pasta instead.*
• *In Rome, the home of this dish, grated cheese is never served with this dish, nor is it seasoned with pepper.*
• *In summer, Romans use fresh chillies, which they grow in pots on their terraces and window ledges. As the chilli is mainly used for flavouring, you could use chilli oil instead.*

Spaghetti with Lemon

This is the dish when you want a quick bite to eat.

Serves 4
350g/12oz dried spaghetti

90ml/6 tbsp extra virgin olive oil
juice of 1 large lemon
2 garlic cloves, cut into very
  thin slivers
salt and ground black pepper

Preparation: 2–3 minutes; Cooking: 15 minutes

1 Cook the pasta in a large pan of lightly salted boiling water for 10–12 minutes, until tender, then drain well and return to the pan. Pour the olive oil and lemon juice over the cooked pasta, sprinkle in the slivers of garlic and add seasoning to taste. Toss the pasta over a medium to high heat for 1–2 minutes. Serve immediately in four warmed bowls.

Minty Courgette Linguine

Courgettes and mint are a great combination and are delicious with pasta.

Serves 4
450g/1lb dried linguine
75ml/5 tbsp garlic-infused olive oil

4 small courgettes (zucchini),
  sliced
1 small bunch of fresh mint,
  roughly chopped
salt and ground black pepper

Preparation: 5 minutes; Cooking: 12–15 minutes

1 Cook the pasta in a large pan of lightly salted boiling water for 10–12 minutes.

2 Meanwhile, heat 45ml/3 tbsp of the oil in a large frying pan and add the courgettes. Fry for 2–3 minutes, stirring occasionally, until they are golden.

3 Drain the pasta well and toss with the courgettes and chopped mint. Season with salt and pepper, drizzle over the remaining oil and serve immediately.

Spaghetti with Garlic Energy 498kcal/2097kJ; Protein 12.6g; Carbohydrate 75.3g, of which sugars 3.4g; Fat 18.3g, of which saturates 2.6g; Cholesterol 0mg; Calcium 27mg; Fibre 3.2g; Sodium 3mg.
Spaghetti with Lemon Energy 448kcal/1886kJ; Protein 10.5g; Carbohydrate 64.9g, of which sugars 3g; Fat 18.1g, of which saturates 2.5g; Cholesterol 0mg; Calcium 22mg; Fibre 2.6g; Sodium 3mg.
Linguine Energy 536kcal/2261kJ; Protein 16.2g; Carbohydrate 86.3g, of which sugars 5.9g; Fat 16.4g, of which saturates 2.3g; Cholesterol 0mg; Calcium 86mg; Fibre 4.4g; Sodium 7mg.

Linguine with Sun-dried Tomato Pesto

Tomato pesto was once a rarity, but is becoming increasingly popular. To make it, sun-dried tomatoes are used instead of basil.

Serves 4
25g/1oz/⅓ cup pine nuts
25g/1oz/⅓ cup freshly grated strong hard cheese
50g/2oz/½ cup sun-dried tomatoes in olive oil
1 garlic clove, roughly chopped
60ml/4 tbsp olive oil
350g/12oz fresh or dried linguine
ground black pepper
coarsely shaved strong hard cheese, to serve
basil leaves, to garnish

Preparation: 5 minutes; Cooking: 5–16 minutes

1 Put the pine nuts in a small non-stick frying pan and toss over a low to medium heat for 1–2 minutes or until lightly toasted and golden.

2 Tip the nuts into a food processor. Add the grated cheese, sun-dried tomatoes and garlic, with pepper to taste. Process until finely chopped. With the machine running, gradually add the olive oil through the feeder tube until it has all been incorporated evenly and the ingredients have formed a smooth-looking paste.

3 Cook the pasta in a large pan of lightly salted boiling water. Dried pasta will take 10–12 minutes, fresh about 3 minutes. Drain well, reserving a little of the water. Tip the pasta into a warmed bowl, add the pesto and a few spoonfuls of the hot water and toss well. Serve immediately garnished with basil and hand round the cheese separately.

> **Cook's Tip**
> You can make this pesto up to 2 days in advance and keep it in the refrigerator. Pour a thin film of olive oil over the pesto in a bowl, then cover the bowl tightly with clear film (plastic wrap).

Pasta with Sun-dried Tomatoes

This is a light, modern pasta dish of the kind served in fashionable restaurants. It is very easy to prepare.

Serves 4–6
45ml/3 tbsp pine nuts
350g/12oz dried paglia e fieno (or two different colours of tagliatelle)
45ml/3 tbsp extra virgin olive oil
30ml/2 tbsp sun-dried tomato paste
2 pieces drained sun-dried tomatoes in olive oil, cut into very thin slivers
40g/1½oz radicchio leaves, finely shredded
4–6 spring onions (scallions), thinly sliced into rings
salt and ground black pepper

Preparation: 3 minutes; Cooking: 13–15 minutes

1 Put the pine nuts in a non-stick frying pan and toss over a low to medium heat for 1–2 minutes or until they are lightly toasted and golden. Remove from the pan and set aside.

2 Cook the pasta in two large pans of lightly salted boiling water for 10–12 minutes, using one pan for each colour to keep them separated.

3 While the pasta is cooking, heat 15ml/1 tbsp of the oil in a medium pan or frying pan. Add the sun-dried tomato paste and the sun-dried tomatoes, then stir in 2 ladlefuls of the water used for cooking the pasta. Simmer until the sauce is slightly reduced, stirring constantly.

4 Mix in the shredded radicchio, then taste and season if necessary. Keep on a low heat. Drain the paglia e fieno, keeping the colours separate, and return the pasta to the pans. Add about 15ml/1 tbsp oil to each pan and toss over a medium to high heat until the pasta is glistening with the oil.

5 Arrange a portion of green and white pasta in each of 4–6 warmed bowls, then spoon the sun-dried tomato and radicchio mixture in the centre. Sprinkle the spring onions and pine nuts over the top and serve immediately. Before eating, each diner should toss the sauce ingredients with the pasta.

Linguine Energy 503kcal/2114kJ; Protein 14.4g; Carbohydrate 66.7g, of which sugars 4.7g; Fat 21.7g, of which saturates 3.4g; Cholesterol 6mg; Calcium 102mg; Fibre 3g; Sodium 98mg.
Pasta Energy 309kcal/1302kJ; Protein 8.6g; Carbohydrate 44.9g, of which sugars 3.6g; Fat 11.8g, of which saturates 1.3g; Cholesterol 0mg; Calcium 23mg; Fibre 2.3g; Sodium 16mg.

Pasta with Tomato & Chilli Sauce

This dish comes from Italy, where it is described as all'arrabbiata. This means 'angry' and it describes the heat that comes from the chilli, but if you serve it to someone who hates spices, it may be directed at you.

Serves 4
500g/1¼ lb sugocasa
  (see Cook's Tip)
2 garlic cloves, crushed
150ml/¼ pint/⅔ cup dry
  white wine
15ml/1 tbsp sun-dried
  tomato paste
1 fresh red chilli
300g/11oz/2¾ cups penne
  or tortiglioni
60ml/4 tbsp finely chopped fresh
  flat leaf parsley
salt and ground black pepper
freshly grated Pecorino cheese,
  to serve

Preparation: 2–3 minutes; Cooking: 12–14 minutes

1 Mix the sugocasa, garlic, wine, sun-dried tomato paste and whole chilli in a pan and bring to the boil. Reduce the heat, cover the pan and leave the mixture to simmer gently, stirring it occasionally with a wooden spoon.

2 Drop the pasta into a large pan of rapidly boiling salted water. Lower the heat and simmer for 10–12 minutes or until the pasta is just tender, retaining a bit of 'bite'.

3 Remove the chilli from the sauce and add 30ml/2 tbsp of the parsley. Taste for seasoning. If you prefer a hotter taste, chop some or all of the chilli and return it to the sauce.

4 Drain the pasta and tip it into a warmed large bowl. Pour the sauce over the pasta and toss to mix. Serve at once, sprinkled with grated Pecorino and the remaining parsley. Offer more grated Pecorino separately, in a small bowl.

Cook's Tip
Sugocasa resembles passata (bottled strained tomatoes), but is a chunkier mixture; it means 'the sauce of the house'.

Broccoli & Chilli Spaghetti

The contrast between the hot chilli and the mild broccoli is delicious and goes perfectly with spaghetti. Extra flavour and texture are added by sprinkling the finished dish with toasted pine nuts and grated or shaved Parmesan cheese just before serving. For a tangy but less spicy result just exclude the chilli from the recipe.

Serves 4
350g/12oz dried spaghetti
450g/1lb broccoli, cut into
  small florets
1 fat red chilli, seeded and
  finely chopped
150ml/¼ pint/⅔ cup garlic-infused
  olive oil
salt and ground black pepper
freshly grated strong hard cheese,
  to serve
handful of toasted pine nuts,
  to serve

Preparation: 2–3 minutes; Cooking: 8–10 minutes

1 Bring a large pan of lightly salted water to the boil. Add the spaghetti and broccoli and cook for 8–10 minutes, until both are tender. Drain thoroughly.

2 Using the back of a fork crush the broccoli roughly, taking care not to mash the spaghetti strands at the same time.

3 Meanwhile, warm the oil and finely chopped chilli in a small pan over a low heat and cook very gently for 5 minutes, taking care not to brown the chilli.

4 Pour the chilli and oil over the spaghetti and broccoli and toss together to combine. Season to taste. Divide between four warmed bowls and serve immediately.

Cook's Tip
Cooking the spaghetti and broccoli in the same pan helps the pasta to absorb more of the vegetable's flavour and essential nutrients. To retain more of the nutrients, reserve a small amount of the cooking water and pour over the dish before tossing together all the ingredients.

Pasta with Tomato Energy 681kcal/2856kJ; Protein 25.1g; Carbohydrate 69.7g, of which sugars 7.7g; Fat 35.5g, of which saturates 19g; Cholesterol 91mg; Calcium 264mg; Fibre 4.1g; Sodium 830mg.
Broccoli Spaghetti Energy 396kcal/1678kJ; Protein 17.3g; Carbohydrate 68.3g, of which sugars 6g; Fat 7.9g, of which saturates 0.8g; Cholesterol 0mg; Calcium 114mg; Fibre 5.6g; Sodium 24mg.

Fettucine all'Alfredo

This simple recipe was invented by a Roman restaurateur called Alfredo, who became famous for serving it with a gold fork and spoon. Since those heady days it has become one of the most popular pasta dishes around.

Serves 4
50g/2oz/¼ cup butter
200ml/7fl oz/scant 1 cup double (heavy) cream
50g/2oz/⅔ cup freshly grated strong hard cheese, plus extra to serve
350g/12oz fresh fettucine
salt and ground black pepper

Preparation: 1–2 minutes; Cooking: 10–12 minutes

1 Melt the butter in a large pan. Add the cream and bring it to the boil. Simmer for 5 minutes, stirring constantly, then add the cheese, with salt and ground black pepper to taste, and turn off the heat under the pan.

2 Bring a large pan of lightly salted water to the boil over high heat. Add the pasta and cook for about 3 minutes, or until the fresh fettucine rises to the surface.

3 Turn the heat under the pan of cream to low. Drain the cooked pasta and add it to the pan all at once. Toss until it is coated in the sauce. Taste for seasoning and stir in more salt and pepper if needed. Serve immediately, with extra cheese handed around separately.

Cook's Tip
A few drops of oil, added to the pan of water in which the fettucine is cooking, will help to prevent it from boiling over.

Variation
The original recipe for Fettucine all'Alfredo did not contain cream, so the version above is already a slight variation. Some cooks add a little cream cheese, which thickens the coating sauce, or even some mashed blue cheese, such as Gorgonzola.

Linguine with Rocket

This fashionable lunch is very quick and easy to make at home. Rocket has an excellent peppery flavour that combines beautifully with the Parmesan, but watercress leaves, which also have a peppery taste, could be used instead.

Serves 4
350g/12oz dried linguine
120ml/4fl oz/½ cup extra virgin olive oil
1 large bunch rocket (arugula), about 150g/5oz, stalks removed, shredded
75g/3oz/1 cup freshly grated strong hard cheese

Preparation: 3–5 minutes; Cooking: 11–14 minutes

1 Cook the pasta in a large pan of lightly salted boiling water for 10–12 minutes, then drain thoroughly.

2 Heat about 60ml/4 tbsp of the olive oil in the pasta pan, then add the drained pasta and rocket. Toss over a medium heat for 1–2 minutes, or until the rocket is just wilted, then remove the pan from the heat.

3 Transfer the pasta and rocket to a large, warmed bowl. Add half the freshly grated cheese and the remaining olive oil. Add a little salt and black pepper to taste.

4 Toss the mixture quickly to mix all the flavours together and ensure the pasta is well coated with the oil. Serve immediately, sprinkled with the remaining cheese.

Cook's Tips
• Linguine is an egg pasta and looks rather like flattened strands of spaghetti.
• Dried pasta cooks in 10–12 minutes, but an even faster result can be obtained by using fresh pasta. Simply add it to a large pan of boiling, lightly salted water, making sure that all the strands are fully submerged, and cook for 2–3 minutes. The pasta is ready when it rises to the top of the pan and is tender to the taste, with a slight firmness in the centre.

Fettucine Energy 697kcal/2912kJ; Protein 16.3g; Carbohydrate 65.8g, of which sugars 3.8g; Fat 42.8g, of which saturates 26g; Cholesterol 108mg; Calcium 199mg; Fibre 2.6g; Sodium 226mg.
Linguine Energy 573kcal/2404kJ; Protein 19g; Carbohydrate 65.4g, of which sugars 3.5g; Fat 28g, of which saturates 6.9g; Cholesterol 19mg; Calcium 311mg; Fibre 3.3g; Sodium 260mg.

Tagliatelle with Vegetable Ribbons

Narrow strips of courgette and carrot mingle well with tagliatelle to resemble coloured pasta. Serve with freshly grated Parmesan cheese handed round separately. Children may prefer grated Cheddar or Edam cheese.

Serves 4

2 large courgettes (zucchini)
2 large carrots
250g/9oz fresh egg tagliatelle
60ml/4 tbsp garlic-flavoured
   olive oil
salt and ground black pepper
freshly grated strong hard cheese,
   to serve

Preparation: 5 minutes; Cooking: 5 minutes

1 With a vegetable peeler, cut the courgettes and carrots into long thin ribbons.

2 Bring a large pan of lightly salted water to the boil, and then add the courgette and carrot ribbons. Bring the water back to the boil and blanch the vegetables for 30 seconds, then remove the courgettes and carrots with a slotted spoon and set them aside in a bowl.

3 Bring the water back to boiling point and cook the pasta for 3 minutes. Drain well and return it to the pan. Add the vegetable ribbons, garlic-flavoured oil and seasoning and toss over a medium to high heat until the pasta and vegetables are glistening with oil. Serve the pasta immediately.

Variation
For a more substantial dish, add 4 vegetarian bacon rashers (strips), grilled (broiled) until crispy, then crumble the rashers on to the pasta.

Cook's Tip
Garlic-flavoured olive oil is used in this dish. Flavoured oils such as chilli or basil are a quick way of adding flavour to pasta.

Farfalle with Gorgonzola Cream

Sweet and simple, this sauce has a nutty tang that comes from the blue cheese. It is also good with long pasta, such as spaghetti, tagliatelle or trenette. Steamed leeks go very well with blue cheeses like Gorgonzola, so cook some separately if you like, and add them when tossing the cooked farfalle with the sauce.

Serves 6

350g/12oz/3 cups dried farfalle
175g/6oz Gorgonzola cheese, any
   rind removed, diced
150ml/¼ pint/¾ cup panna da
   cucina or double (heavy) cream
pinch of sugar
10ml/2 tsp finely chopped fresh
   sage, plus fresh sage leaves
   (some whole, some shredded)
   to garnish
salt and ground black pepper

Preparation: 5 minutes; Cooking: 12–14 minutes

1 Cook the pasta in a large pan of lightly salted boiling water for 10–12 minutes.

2 Meanwhile, put the Gorgonzola and cream in a medium pan. Add the sugar and plenty of ground black pepper and heat gently, stirring frequently, until the cheese has melted. Remove the pan from the heat and let the mixture cool slightly.

3 Drain the cooked pasta well and return it to the pan in which it was cooked. Pour the sauce into the pan with the pasta and gently mix the ingredients together.

4 Add the chopped sage to the pasta and toss over a medium heat until the pasta is evenly coated. Taste for seasoning, adding salt if necessary, then divide among four warmed bowls. Garnish each portion with sage and serve immediately.

Variation
Pine nuts, which are sometimes called pignoli, make a lovely addition to this dish. They can be added just as they are, but will taste even better if spread out in a grill (broiler) pan and toasted under a hot grill for a couple of minutes until browned.

Tagliatelle Energy 397kcal/1663kJ; Protein 11.5g; Carbohydrate 52.4g, of which sugars 8.3g; Fat 17.1g, of which saturates 3.3g; Cholesterol 19mg; Calcium 80mg; Fibre 4.8g; Sodium 127mg.
Farfalle Energy 423kcal/1773kJ; Protein 13.4g; Carbohydrate 43.7g, of which sugars 2.4g; Fat 22.9g, of which saturates 14.1g; Cholesterol 56mg; Calcium 169mg; Fibre 1.7g; Sodium 363mg.

Quick Risotto

This is rather a cheat's risotto as it defies all the rules that insist the stock is added gradually. Instead, the rice is cooked quickly in a conventional way, and the other ingredients are simply thrown in at the end. Despite the unconventional cooking method it tastes just as good as a traditional risotto. Chopped cooked ham can be added at the last minute for meat eaters.

Serves 3–4
275g/10oz/1½ cups risotto rice
1 litre/1¾ pints/4 cups
    vegetable stock
115g/4oz/1 cup mozzarella
    cheese, cut into small cubes
2 egg yolks
30ml/2 tbsp freshly grated strong
    hard cheese
30ml/2 tbsp chopped fresh basil
salt and ground black pepper
fresh basil leaves, to garnish
freshly grated strong hard cheese,
    to serve

Preparation: 3–4 minutes; Cooking: 16–17 minutes

1 Put the rice in a pan. Pour in the stock, bring to the boil and then cover and simmer for 16–17 minutes until the rice is tender but retains a bit of bite in the centre of the grain.

2 Remove the pan from the heat and quickly stir in the mozzarella, egg yolks, grated cheese and basil. Season well with salt and pepper.

3 Cover the pan and stand for 2–3 minutes to allow the cheese to melt, then stir again. Pile into warmed serving bowls and serve immediately, with extra grated cheese and basil leaves.

Cook's Tip
Making this in the conventional way will not take much longer. Have the stock simmering in a pan. Instead of using egg yolks, melt 50g/2oz/¼ cup butter in a heavy pan. Stir in the rice. Add a ladleful of stock and stir until it has been absorbed. Continue in this fashion, stirring all the time, until all the stock has been added. When the rice is tender, after 18–20 minutes, stir in the remaining ingredients and proceed as in the main recipe.

Two Cheese Risotto

This undeniably rich and creamy risotto is just the thing to serve on cold winter evenings when everyone needs warming up. This is a very sociable dish. Invite guests into the kitchen for a chat while you cook.

Serves 3–4
7.5ml/1½ tsp olive oil
50g/2oz/4 tbsp butter
1 onion, finely chopped
1 garlic clove, crushed
275g/10oz/1½ cups risotto rice
175ml/6fl oz/¾ cup dry
    white wine
1 litre/1¾ pints/4 cups
    vegetable stock
75g/3oz/¾ cup fontina
    cheese, cubed
50g/2oz/⅔ cup freshly grated
    strong hard cheese, plus extra
    shavings to serve
salt and ground black pepper

Preparation: 2 minutes; Cooking: 18 minutes

1 Heat the olive oil with half the butter in a pan and gently fry the onion and garlic for 3 minutes until soft. Add the rice and cook, stirring all the time, until the grains are coated in fat and have become slightly translucent around the edges.

2 Stir in the wine. Cook, stirring, until the liquid has been absorbed, then add a ladleful of hot stock. Stir until the stock has been absorbed, then add the remaining stock in the same way, waiting for each quantity of stock to be absorbed before adding more, and stirring all the time.

3 When the rice is half cooked, after about 9 minutes, stir in the fontina cheese, and continue cooking and adding stock. Keep stirring the rice all the time.

4 When the risotto is creamy and the grains are tender but still have a bit of bite, stir in the remaining butter and the grated cheese. Season, then remove the pan from the heat, cover and leave to rest for 1 minute before spooning into a large bowl or on to individual plates and serving. Shave a little strong hard cheese over each portion and put the remaining cheese on the table with a cheese shaver so guests can add more cheese later, if they like.

Quick Risotto Energy 405kcal/1692kJ; Protein 18.3g; Carbohydrate 55.1g, of which sugars 0.2g; Fat 12g, of which saturates 6.5g; Cholesterol 136mg; Calcium 221mg; Fibre 0g; Sodium 425mg.
Two Cheese Risotto Energy 547kcal/2273kJ; Protein 15.1g; Carbohydrate 56.4g, of which sugars 1.2g; Fat 25.1g, of which saturates 13.8g; Cholesterol 57mg; Calcium 312mg; Fibre 0.2g; Sodium 350mg.

Pink Grapefruit & Avocado Salad

Smooth, creamy avocado, zesty pink grapefruit and peppery rocket are perfect partners in this attractive, refreshing salad. The chilli oil adds a spicy note.

Serves 4
2 pink grapefruit
2 ripe avocados
90g/3½ oz rocket (arugula)
30ml/2 tbsp chilli oil
salt and ground black pepper

Preparation: 8 minutes; Cooking: 0 minutes

1 Slice the top and bottom off one of the grapefruit, then cut off all the peel and pith from around the side. Working over a small bowl to catch the juices, cut out the segments from between the membranes and place them in a separate bowl.

2 Squeeze any juices remaining in the membranes into the juice bowl, then discard them. Repeat with the remaining grapefruit.

3 Halve, stone (pit) and peel the avocados. Slice the flesh and add it to the grapefruit segments. Whisk a little salt and then the chilli oil into the grapefruit juice.

4 Pile the rocket leaves on to four serving plates and top with the grapefruit segments and avocado. Pour over the dressing, making sure it is evenly distributed, and serve.

Cook's Tips
• Avocados turn brown quickly when exposed to the air, but the acidic grapefruit juice will prevent this. Combine the ingredients as soon as the avocados have been sliced.
• Rocket (arugula) is one of the easiest herbs to grow. Sow successive plantings for a continuous supply of the leaves.

Variation
Pink grapefruit are tangy but not too sharp for this salad, alternatively you could try large oranges for a sweeter flavour.

Salad of Wild Greens & Olives

This simple salad takes only a few minutes to put together. Use as wide a variety of greens as you can find, matching sweet flavours with a few bitter leaves for flavour accent.

Serves 4
115g/4oz wild rocket (arugula)
1 packet mixed salad leaves
¼ white cabbage, thinly sliced
1 cucumber, sliced
1 small red onion, chopped

2–3 garlic cloves, chopped
3–5 tomatoes, cut into wedges
1 green (bell) pepper, seeded and sliced
2–3 mint sprigs, sliced or torn
15–30ml/1–2 tbsp chopped fresh parsley and/or tarragon or dill
pinch of dried oregano or thyme
45ml/3 tbsp extra virgin olive oil
juice of ½ lemon
15ml/1 tbsp red wine vinegar
15–20 black olives
salt and ground black pepper
cottage cheese, to serve

Preparation: 6 minutes; Cooking: 0 minutes

1 In a large salad bowl, put the rocket, mixed salad leaves, sliced white cabbage, sliced cucumber, chopped onion and chopped garlic. Toss gently with your fingers to combine the leaves and vegetables.

2 Arrange the tomatoes, pepper, mint, fresh and dried herbs, salt and pepper on top of the greens and vegetables. Drizzle over the oil, lemon juice and vinegar, stud with the olives and serve with a bowl of cottage cheese.

Variation
This is traditionally served with labneh or yogurt cheese, but tastes good with cottage cheese too. Alternatively, try it with feta, either placing a slab on the salad, or adding cubes.

Cook's Tip
Try to find mixed salad leaves that include varieties such as lamb's lettuce, purslane and mizuna.

Pink Grapefruit Energy 174kcal/719kJ; Protein 2.2g; Carbohydrate 6.8g, of which sugars 6g; Fat 15.4g, of which saturates 2.9g; Cholesterol 0mg; Calcium 62mg; Fibre 3.2g; Sodium 37mg.
Wild Greens Energy 150kcal/619kJ; Protein 3.3g; Carbohydrate 10.4g, of which sugars 9.8g; Fat 10.7g, of which saturates 1.6g; Cholesterol 0mg; Calcium 106mg; Fibre 4.2g; Sodium 338mg.

Turnip Salad in Sour Cream

Often neglected, turnips make an unusual and very tasty accompaniment when prepared in this simple way. For the best results, choose young, tender turnips of the type the French call 'navets' and slice them thinly.

Serves 4
2–4 young, tender turnips, peeled
$^1/_4$–$^1/_2$ onion, finely chopped
2–3 drops white wine vinegar, or
   to taste
60–90ml/4–6 tbsp sour cream
salt and ground black pepper
chopped fresh parsley or paprika,
   to garnish

Preparation: 5 minutes; Cooking: 0 minutes

1 Thinly slice or coarsely grate the turnips. Alternatively, thinly slice half the turnips and grate the ones that remain. Put in a bowl. Add the onion, vinegar, salt and pepper, toss together then stir in the sour cream. Serve chilled, garnished with a sprinkling of chopped fresh parsley or paprika.

Mushroom Salad

This simple refreshing salad is often served as part of a selection of vegetable salads, or crudités.

Serves 4
175g/6oz button (white)
   mushrooms, trimmed
grated rind and juice of
   1$^1/_2$ lemons
about 30–45ml/2–3 tbsp crème
   fraîche or sour cream
salt and ground white pepper
15ml/1 tbsp chopped fresh
   chives or sliced radishes,
   to garnish

Preparation: 5 minutes; Cooking: 0 minutes

1 Slice the mushrooms thinly and place in a bowl. In a separate bowl mix the lemon rind and juice and the cream, adding a little more cream if needed. Spoon over the mushrooms.

2 Stir gently to mix, then season with salt and pepper. Sprinkle the salad with chopped chives before serving.

Green Leaf Salad with Capers & Stuffed Olives

The best time to make this refreshing salad is in the summer when tomatoes are at their sweetest and full of flavour. It makes a colourful addition to the table.

Serves 4
4 tomatoes
$^1/_2$ cucumber
1 bunch spring onions (scallions),
   trimmed
1 bunch watercress
8 stuffed olives
30ml/2 tbsp drained capers

For the dressing
30ml/2 tbsp red wine vinegar
5ml/1 tsp paprika
2.5ml/$^1/_2$ tsp ground cumin
1 garlic clove, crushed
75 ml/5 tbsp olive oil
salt and ground black pepper

Preparation: 10 minutes; Cooking: 0 minutes

1 Peel the tomatoes, if you like, although this is not essential, and finely dice the flesh. Put them in a salad bowl.

2 Peel the cucumber, dice it finely and add it to the tomatoes. Chop half the spring onions, add them to the salad bowl and mix lightly. Break the watercress into sprigs. Add to the tomato mixture, with the olives and capers.

3 To make the dressing, mix the wine vinegar, paprika, cumin and garlic in a bowl. Whisk in the oil and add salt and pepper to taste. Pour over the salad and toss lightly. Serve immediately with the remaining spring onions.

> **Cook's Tip**
> *Stuffed olives are delicious in a salad, and also prove popular when set out in a bowl to serve with drinks. There are several different types on sale, generally using green olives. Fillings include anchovies, pimiento, cheese – including blue cheese – garlic, almonds and lemon. For this recipe, the pimiento or anchovy-stuffed olives would be best.*

Turnip Salad Energy 48kcal/198kJ; Protein 1.1g; Carbohydrate 4.1g, of which sugars 3.7g; Fat 3.2g, of which saturates 1.9g; Cholesterol 9mg; Calcium 42mg; Fibre 1.4g; Sodium 14mg.
Mushroom Salad Energy 22kcal/93kJ; Protein 1.1g; Carbohydrate 0.6g, of which sugars 0.5g; Fat 1.8g, of which saturates 1g; Cholesterol 5mg; Calcium 17mg; Fibre 0.7g; Sodium 7mg
Green Leaf Salad Energy 167kcal/692kJ; Protein 2.2g; Carbohydrate 4.3g, of which sugars 4.3g; Fat 15.8g, of which saturates 2.4g; Cholesterol 0mg; Calcium 72mg; Fibre 2.3g; Sodium 305mg.

Halloumi & Grape Salad

In Eastern Europe, firm salty halloumi cheese is often served fried for breakfast or supper. In this recipe it is tossed with sweet, juicy grapes which really complement its distinctive sweet and salty flavour.

Serves 4
150g/5oz mixed green
  salad leaves
75g/3oz seedless grapes

250g/9oz halloumi cheese
45ml/3 tbsp olive oil
fresh young thyme leaves or dill,
  to garnish

For the dressing
60ml/4 tbsp olive oil
15ml/1 tbsp lemon juice
2.5ml/$\frac{1}{2}$ tsp caster (superfine)
  sugar
salt and ground black pepper
5ml/1 tsp chopped fresh thyme
  or dill

Preparation: 2 minutes; Cooking: 3–4 minutes

1 To make the dressing, mix together the olive oil, lemon juice and sugar. Season with salt and ground black pepper. Stir in the thyme or dill and set aside.

2 Toss together the salad leaves and the green and black grapes, then transfer to a large serving plate.

3 Thinly slice the cheese. Heat the oil in a frying pan. Add the cheese and fry briefly until turning golden on the underside. Turn with a fish slice or metal spatula and cook the other side.

4 Arrange the cheese over the salad. Pour over the dressing and garnish with thyme or dill.

> **Variations**
> • Add a few fresh mint leaves to the salad leaves, or some young sorrel leaves. Sorrel has a lovely lemony flavour but is high in oxalic acid, so don't use too much.
> • Substitute physalis for the grapes. These little golden fruits have a delicious sweet-sour flavour which would be an excellent foil for the salty halloumi cheese.

Warm Halloumi & Fennel Salad

Halloumi is a robust cheese that holds its shape when cooked on a griddle or barbecue. During cooking it acquires the distinctive griddle marks that look so effective. It tastes good with the aniseed-flavoured fennel and the herbs.

Serves 4
200g/7oz halloumi cheese,
  thickly sliced
2 fennel bulbs, trimmed and
  thinly sliced
30ml/2 tbsp roughly chopped
  fresh oregano
45ml/3 tbsp lemon-infused olive oil
salt and ground black pepper

Preparation: 13 minutes; Cooking: 6 minutes

1 Put the halloumi, fennel and oregano in a bowl and drizzle over the lemon-infused oil. Season with salt and black pepper to taste.

2 Cover the bowl with clear film (plastic wrap) and set aside for 10 minutes.

3 Place the halloumi and fennel on a hot griddle pan or over the barbecue, reserving the marinade, and cook for about 3 minutes on each side, until charred.

4 Divide the halloumi and fennel among four serving plates and drizzle over the reserved marinade. Serve immediately.

> **Variation**
> Instead of fennel, use young heads of chicory (Belgian endive). Remove any discoloured leaves. Trim the ends slightly. Using a small knife, cut out the bitter core at the base of each endive head. Slice the endive heads thinly.

> **Cook's Tip**
> If you have time, chill the halloumi and fennel mixture for about 2 hours before cooking, so it becomes infused with the dressing.

Halloumi and Grape Energy 215kcal/889kJ; Protein 10.2g; Carbohydrate 1.8g, of which sugars 1.7g; Fat 18.6g, of which saturates 8.1g; Cholesterol 29mg; Calcium 205mg; Fibre 2.4g; Sodium 209mg.
Warm Halloumi Energy 212kcal/876kJ; Protein 10g; Carbohydrate 1.4g, of which sugars 1.3g; Fat 18.6g, of which saturates 8.1g; Cholesterol 29mg; Calcium 199mg; Fibre 1.8g; Sodium 206mg.

Warm Broad Bean & Feta Salad

This recipe is loosely based on a typical medley of fresh-tasting Greek salad ingredients – broad beans, tomatoes and feta cheese. It's lovely as a starter, served warm or cold. It is the sort of dish that would go down very well at a party, so next time you are invited to one of those occasions where every guest brings a contribution, this would be an ideal choice.

Serves 4–6
900g/2lb broad beans, shelled, or 350g/12oz shelled frozen beans
60ml/4 tbsp olive oil
75g/3oz plum tomatoes, halved, or quartered if large
4 garlic cloves, crushed
115g/4oz firm feta cheese, cut into large, even-sized chunks
45ml/3 tbsp chopped fresh dill, plus extra to garnish
12 black olives
salt and ground black pepper

Preparation: 4 minutes; Cooking: 6–8 minutes

1 Cook the fresh or frozen broad beans in lightly salted boiling water until just tender. Drain and refresh, then set aside.

2 Meanwhile, heat the oil in a heavy frying pan and add the tomatoes and garlic. Cook until the tomatoes are beginning to colour and the garlic is pungent.

3 Add the feta to the pan and toss the ingredients together for 1 minute. Mix with the drained beans, dill, olives and salt and pepper. Serve garnished with chopped dill.

Variations
• For a special treat, pop the shelled broad beans out of their skins and use only the bright green beans inside. This is a bit of a fiddly business, and doesn't yield much in terms of weight of beans, but as a bonus, the appearance and flavour is superb.
• Instead of broad beans, use extra-fine green beans, French beans or even runner beans. A mixture of green and yellow beans would look good, when the latter are in season.
• Use tiny cocktail tomatoes instead of plum tomatoes.

Warm Salad with Poached Eggs

Soft poached eggs, chilli, hot croûtons and cool, crisp salad leaves make a lively and unusual combination. This simple salad is perfect for a mid-week supper. Poached eggs are delicious with salad leaves as the yolk runs out when the eggs are pierced and combines with the dressing in the most delightful way.

Serves 2
½ small loaf wholemeal (whole-wheat) bread
45ml/3 tbsp chilli oil
2 eggs
115g/4oz mixed salad leaves
45ml/3 tbsp extra virgin olive oil
2 garlic cloves, crushed
15ml/1 tbsp balsamic or sherry vinegar
50g/2oz strong hard cheese, shaved
ground black pepper

Preparation: 2–3 minutes; Cooking: 10–12 minutes

1 Carefully cut the crust from the wholemeal loaf and discard. Cut the bread into neat slices and then into 2.5cm/1in cubes.

2 Heat the chilli oil in a large frying pan. Add the bread cubes and cook for about 5 minutes, tossing the cubes occasionally, until they are crisp and golden brown all over.

3 Meanwhile, bring a pan of water to the boil. Break each egg into a measuring jug (cup) and carefully slide into the water, one at a time.

4 Gently poach the eggs in the simmering water for about 4 minutes until they are lightly cooked.

5 Meanwhile, divide the salad leaves between two plates. Using a slotted spoon, remove the croûtons from the pan and arrange them over the leaves.

6 Wipe the pan clean with kitchen paper. Then heat the olive oil in the pan, add the garlic and vinegar and cook over high heat for 1 minute. Pour the warm dressing over the salads.

7 Place a poached egg on each salad. Top with thin cheese shavings and a little ground black pepper. Serve immediately.

Warm Broad Bean Energy 175kcal/727kJ; Protein 7.9g; Carbohydrate 8g, of which sugars 2g; Fat 12.6g, of which saturates 3.9g; Cholesterol 13mg; Calcium 109mg; Fibre 4.3g; Sodium 471mg.
Warm Salad Energy 697kcal/2907kJ; Protein 25.9g; Carbohydrate 41.3g, of which sugars 2.8g; Fat 49g, of which saturates 11.5g; Cholesterol 215mg; Calcium 408mg; Fibre 6.3g; Sodium 914mg.

Stir-fried Noodles with Beansprouts

A classic Chinese noodle combination that makes a marvellous accompaniment to a variety of both Eastern and Western dishes.

Serves 4
175g/6oz dried egg noodles
15ml/1 tbsp vegetable oil

1 garlic clove, finely chopped
1 small onion, halved and sliced
225g/8oz/2⅔ cups beansprouts
1 small red (bell) pepper, seeded
    and cut into strips
1 small green (bell) pepper,
    seeded and cut into strips
2.5ml/½ tsp salt
1.5ml/¼ tsp ground white pepper
30ml/2 tbsp light soy sauce

Preparation: 5 minutes; Cooking: 9–13 minutes

1 Bring a pan of water to the boil. Cook the noodles for 4 minutes until just tender or according to the instructions on the packet. Drain, refresh under cold water and drain again.

2 Heat the oil in a non-stick frying pan or wok. When the oil is very hot, add the garlic, stir briefly, then add the onion slices. Cook, stirring, for 1 minute, then add the beansprouts and peppers. Stir-fry for 2–3 minutes.

3 Stir in the cooked noodles and toss over the heat, using two spatulas or wooden spoons, for 2–3 minutes or until the ingredients are well mixed and have heated through.

4 Add the salt, pepper and soy sauce and stir thoroughly before serving the noodle mixture in heated bowls.

> **Cook's Tip**
> *Non-stick woks are a good way of minimizing the amount of fat required for cooking. However, they cannot be heated to the very high temperatures that stir-frying meat usually requires. This dish is an ideal candidate for an electric wok. Preheat it before adding the oil, pouring it around the inner rim so that it flows down to coat the surface. Use a high temperature for the initial stir-frying, but turn it down when reheating the noodles.*

Spicy Avocado Salsa

Nachos or tortilla chips are the perfect accompaniment for this classic Mexican dip, which not only tastes deliciously fresh but also takes just minutes to prepare. It makes a very good filling for cocktail tomatoes which have been halved and hollowed out.

Serves 4
2 ripe avocados
2 fresh red chillies, seeded
1 garlic clove
1 shallot
30ml/2 tbsp olive oil, plus extra
    to serve
juice of 1 lemon
salt
flat leaf parsley, to garnish

Preparation: 5 minutes; Cooking: 0 minutes

1 Halve the avocados, remove their stones (pits) and, using a spoon, scoop out their flesh into a bowl. Mash the flesh well with a large fork or a potato masher.

2 Finely chop the chillies, garlic and shallot, then stir into the mashed avocado with the olive oil and lemon juice. Taste the mixture and add a little salt if required.

3 Spoon the mixture into a small serving bowl. Drizzle a little olive oil over the surface and scatter with a few flat leaf parsley leaves. Serve immediately, or the guacamole may discolour.

> **Variations**
> *• Add a diced tomato to the guacamole for extra colour and flavour, or stir in some chopped sun-dried tomatoes.*
> *• Use the juice of 2 limes instead of the lemon, if you prefer.*

> **Cook's Tip**
> *The lemon juice prevents the avocado flesh from discolouring once it is exposed to the air. However, even with lemon juice in a recipe, it is still sensible to prepare avocado dishes shortly before they are to be eaten rather than hours in advance.*

Noodles Energy 244kcal/1030kJ; Protein 8g; Carbohydrate 39.9g, of which sugars 7.8g; Fat 7g, of which saturates 1.5g; Cholesterol 13mg; Calcium 34mg; Fibre 3.5g; Sodium 352mg.
Avocado Salsa Energy 151kcal/623kJ; Protein 1.2g; Carbohydrate 2.4g, of which sugars 1.3g; Fat 15.2g, of which saturates 2.9g; Cholesterol 0mg; Calcium 10mg; Fibre 2g; Sodium 4mg.

Yogurt Dip

This is a less rich version of a classic mayonnaise and is much easier to make. It tastes quite creamy, thanks to the small amount of mayonnaise in the mixture, and serves not only as a dip but also as a salad dressing.

Makes about 210ml/7fl oz/ scant 1 cup
150ml/¼ pint/⅔ cup natural (plain) yogurt
30ml/2 tbsp mayonnaise
30ml/2 tbsp milk
15ml/1 tbsp chopped fresh parsley
15ml/1 tbsp chopped fresh chives

Preparation: 2 minutes; Cooking: 0 minutes

1 Put all the ingredients together in a bowl. Season to taste with salt and ground black pepper and mix well. If not serving immediately, cover the bowl and place the dip in the refrigerator until required.

Artichoke & Cumin Dip

This dip is so easy to make and is unbelievably tasty. Serve with olives, hummus and wedges of pitta bread as part of a selection of snacks for an informal party in the summertime.

Serves 4
2 x 400g/14oz cans artichoke hearts, drained
2 garlic cloves, peeled
2.5ml/½ tsp ground cumin
olive oil
salt and ground black pepper

Preparation: 2 minutes; Cooking: 0 minutes

1 Put the artichoke hearts in a food processor with the garlic and ground cumin, and add a generous drizzle of olive oil. Process to a smooth purée and season with plenty of salt and ground black pepper to taste.

2 Spoon the purée into a serving bowl and serve with an extra drizzle of olive oil swirled on the top and slices of warm pitta bread or wholemeal (whole-wheat) toast fingers and carrot sticks for dipping.

Muhammara

This thick, roasted red pepper and walnut purée is popular in the Middle East. Serve it as a dip with spears of cos or romaine lettuce, wedges of pitta bread and chunks of tomato.

Serves 4
1½ slices Granary (whole-wheat) bread, day-old and toasted
3 red (bell) peppers, roasted, skinned and chopped
2 very mild chillies, roasted, skinned and chopped
115g/4oz/1 cup walnut pieces
3–4 garlic cloves, chopped
15–30ml/1–2 tbsp balsamic vinegar or pomegranate molasses
juice of ½ lemon
2.5–5ml/½–1 tsp ground cumin
2.5ml/½ tsp sugar, or to taste
105ml/7 tbsp olive oil, preferably extra virgin
salt

Preparation: 8 minutes; Cooking: 0 minutes

1 Break the Granary bread into small pieces and place in a food processor or blender with all the remaining ingredients except the extra virgin olive oil. Blend together until the ingredients are finely chopped.

2 With the motor running, slowly drizzle the extra virgin olive oil into the food processor or blender and process until the mixture forms a smooth paste. Tip the muhammara into a serving dish. Serve at room temperature.

Variation
For a quick and easy variation on the muhammara theme, make red pepper hummus. Drain a 400g/14oz can of chickpeas in a colander, rinse them gently under cold water and drain again. Tip into the bowl of a food processor. Scoop out 2 roasted red peppers from a jar or can, remove any seeds, then add them to the food processor with 1 crushed garlic clove, 15ml/1 tbsp tahini, 2.5ml/½ tsp ground cumin and 2.5ml/½ tsp mild chilli powder. Whizz these ingredients together, then scrape the mixture into a bowl and add salt, pepper and lemon juice to taste. Serve at room temperature.

Yogurt Dip Energy 315kcal/1308kJ; Protein 9.9g; Carbohydrate 14g, of which sugars 13.7g; Fat 25.1g, of which saturates 4.5g; Cholesterol 26mg; Calcium 383mg; Fibre 1.5g; Sodium 282mg.
Artichoke Dip Energy 76kcal/315kJ; Protein 1.6g; Carbohydrate 3.9g, of which sugars 3.5g; Fat 6.2g, of which saturates 1g; Cholesterol 0mg; Calcium 18mg; Fibre 3.5g; Sodium 4mg.
Muhammara Energy 444kcal/1833kJ; Protein 6.8g; Carbohydrate 15.5g, of which sugars 9.9g; Fat 39.8g, of which saturates 4.6g; Cholesterol 0mg; Calcium 62mg; Fibre 3.7g; Sodium 69mg.

Chocolate & Banana Fool

This delicious dessert has
a lovely flavour. It is quite
rich, so it is a good idea to
serve it with some dessert
biscuits, such as shortbread,
biscotti or vanilla wafers.
Serves 4

115g/4oz plain (semisweet)
  chocolate, broken into
  small pieces
300ml/½ pint/1¼ cups ready-
  made fresh custard
2 bananas

Preparation: 3 minutes; Cooking: 2 minutes

1 Put the chocolate pieces in a heatproof bowl and melt in the
microwave on high power for 1–2 minutes. Stir, then set aside. If
you do not have a microwave, put the chocolate in a heatproof
bowl and place it over a pan of water that has boiled and then
been removed from the heat. Leave until melted, stirring
frequently to ensure that the liquid chocolate is perfectly smooth.

2 Pour the custard into a bowl and gently fold in the melted
chocolate to make a rippled effect.

3 Peel and slice the bananas and stir these into the chocolate
and custard mixture. Spoon into four glasses. If you have time,
chill for at least 30 minutes before serving.

> **Variation**
> *For a lovely contrast in texture, fry wholemeal (whole-wheat)
> breadcrumbs in butter with a little sugar until crisp. When cool,
> layer the crunchy crumbs with the chocolate custard and fruit.*

> **Cook's Tip**
> *Good-quality bought custard is ideal for this dessert. Don't be
> tempted to use anything but the best chocolate, though, or the
> flavour will be compromised. Look for a bar that contains at
> least 70 per cent cocoa solids. A flavoured chocolate such as
> pistachio or orange takes the dessert into another dimension.*

Lemon Posset

This old-fashioned dessert
was once considered a
remedy for the common
cold. It is certainly worth
suffering a sniffle if it means
you get to sample its superb
citrus and cream flavour.

Serves 4
600ml/1 pint/2½ cups double
  (heavy) cream
175g/6oz/scant 1 cup caster
  (superfine) sugar
grated rind and juice of
  2 unwaxed lemons

Preparation: 2 minutes; Cooking: 8–10 minutes

1 Pour the cream into a heavy pan. Add the sugar and heat
gently until the sugar has dissolved, then bring to the boil,
stirring constantly. Add the lemon juice and rind, reserving a
little of the rind for decoration, and stir constantly over a
medium heat until it thickens.

2 Pour the mixture into four heatproof serving glasses. Cool,
then chill in the refrigerator until just set. Serve the posset
decorated with a few strands of lemon rind, and with a
selection of dessert biscuits (cookies), if you like. Rich, buttery
shortbread is ideal.

> **Variation**
> *To intensify the lemon flavour of this lovely old-fashioned
> dessert even more, swirl a spoonful of lemon curd or lemon
> cheese on the surface just before serving. Physalis make a
> suitable and very stylish accompaniment.*

Apple & Rose Petal Snow

This is a lovely, light and
refreshing dessert, which is
ideal to make when the
trees in the orchards are
groaning with apples. The
rose petals give a delicate
fragrance, which is
heightened by the use of
rose water. Other edible
petals such as honeysuckle,
lavender and geranium could
also be used.

Serves 4
2 large cooking apples
150ml/¼ pint/⅔ cup thick
  apple juice
30ml/1 tbsp rose water
2 egg whites
75g/3oz/generous ⅓ cup caster
  sugar, or to taste
a few rose petals from an
  unsprayed rose
crisp biscuits (cookies) or brandy
  snaps, to serve

Preparation: 5 minutes; Cooking: 3–4 minutes

1 Peel and chop the apples and cook with the apple juice until
soft. Strain, then add the rose water and leave to cool.

2 Whisk the egg whites until peaking, then gently whisk in the
sugar. Gently fold together the apple and egg whites. Stir in
most of the rose petals.

3 Spoon the snow into four glasses and chill. Serve topped
with the remaining petals and crisp biscuits or brandy snaps.

Chocolate Fool Energy 268kcal/1127kJ; Protein 4.1g; Carbohydrate 42.1g, of which sugars 38.1g; Fat 9.6g, of which saturates 4.9g; Cholesterol 3mg; Calcium 81mg; Fibre 1.4g; Sodium 33mg.
Lemon Posset Energy 917kcal/3801kJ; Protein 2.7g; Carbohydrate 48.5g, of which sugars 48.5g; Fat 80.6g, of which saturates 50.1g; Cholesterol 206mg; Calcium 98mg; Fibre 0g; Sodium 36mg.
Apple and Rose Petal Snow Energy 113kcal/483kJ; Protein 1.7g; Carbohydrate 28.1g, of which sugars 28.1g; Fat 0.1g, of which saturates 0g; Cholesterol 0mg; Calcium 16mg; Fibre 0.9g; Sodium 33mg.

Rhubarb & Ginger Trifles

Choose a good-quality jar of rhubarb compote for this recipe; try to find one with large, chunky pieces of fruit. Alternatively, for even more zing, use rhubarb and ginger jam, or whole-fruit apricot jam.

Serves 4
12 gingernut biscuits (gingersnaps)
50ml/2fl oz/¼ cup rhubarb compote
450ml/¾ pint/scant 2 cups extra thick double (heavy) cream

Preparation: 3–4 minutes; Cooking: 0 minutes

1 Put the ginger biscuits in a strong plastic bag and knot it tightly to seal. Bash the biscuits with a rolling pin or meat mallet until roughly crushed. The biscuits can also be crumbed in a food processor but use the pulse button and watch closely as it is important they are only crushed and not reduced to fine crumbs.

2 Set aside two tablespoons of crushed biscuits in a bowl and divide the rest among four glasses.

3 Spoon the rhubarb compote on top of the crushed biscuits, then top with the cream. Place in the refrigerator and chill for about 30 minutes.

4 To finish, sprinkle the reserved crushed biscuits over the trifles and serve immediately.

Variations
• Try this with hazelnut biscuits (cookies) and gooseberry compote for a delicious change.
• Instead of using individual glasses, use a straight-sided glass bowl. Dribble ginger wine over the layer of crushed biscuits.
• Add a layer of custard. Good-quality bought custard is fine.
• Use choc chip cookies instead of gingernuts (gingersnaps) and crumble a chocolate flake bar over the top of the dessert.
• Amaretti biscuits or ratafias also work well and are particularly good with apricot compote.

Blueberry Meringue Crumble

Imagine the most appealing flavours of a blueberry meringue dessert – fresh tangy fruit, crisp sugary meringue and vanilla-scented cream – all served in a tall glass for easy eating. For a patriotic pudding, add a layer of cooked cranberries or raspberries and celebrate the red, white and blue. This is a fun way to mark a national day.

Serves 3–4
150g/5oz/1¼ cups fresh blueberries, plus extra to decorate
15ml/1 tbsp icing (confectioners') sugar
250ml/8fl oz/1 cup vanilla iced yogurt
200ml/7fl oz/scant 1 cup full cream (whole) milk
30ml/2 tbsp lime juice
75g/3oz meringues, lightly crushed

Preparation: 4 minutes; Cooking: 0 minutes

1 Put the blueberries and sugar in a blender or food processor with 60ml/4 tbsp water and blend until smooth, scraping the mixture down from the side once or twice, if necessary.

2 Transfer the purée to a small bowl and rinse out the blender or food processor bowl to get rid of any remaining juice.

3 Put the iced yogurt, milk and lime juice in the blender and process until thoroughly combined. Add half of the crushed meringues and process again until smooth.

4 Carefully pour alternate layers of the milkshake, blueberry syrup and the remaining crushed meringues into tall glasses, finishing with a few chunky pieces of meringue.

5 Drizzle any remaining blueberry syrup over the tops of the meringues and decorate with a few extra blueberries. Serve.

Variation
Iced yogurt is used to provide a slightly lighter note than ice cream, but there's nothing to stop you using ice cream instead.

Ginger Trifles Energy 695kcal/2874kJ; Protein 3.6g; Carbohydrate 27.1g, of which sugars 14.1g; Fat 64.3g, of which saturates 39.4g; Cholesterol 154mg; Calcium 98mg; Fibre 0.6g; Sodium 124mg.
Meringue Crumble Energy 164kcal/691kJ; Protein 6.2g; Carbohydrate 30.8g, of which sugars 30.8g; Fat 2.7g, of which saturates 1.6g; Cholesterol 8mg; Calcium 197mg; Fibre 1.2g; Sodium 96mg.

Pineapple Baked Alaska

Most children love the
surprise of this classic
pudding – hot meringue with
ice-cold ice cream inside.
Here's a new variation, with
coconut and pineapple.

Serves 3–4
3 large (US extra large)
   egg whites
150g/5oz/¾ cup caster
   (superfine) sugar

25g/1oz desiccated (dry
   unsweetened shredded)
   coconut
175–225g/6–8oz piece of ready-
   made cake, such as ginger
   or chocolate
6 slices ripe, peeled pineapple
500ml/17fl oz/2¼ cups vanilla
   ice cream, in a brick
a few cherries or figs,
   to decorate

Preparation: 5 minutes; Cooking: 5–7 minutes

1 Preheat the oven to 230°C/450°F/Gas 8. Whisk the egg
whites in a grease-free bowl until stiff, then whisk in the sugar
until the mixture is stiff and glossy. Fold in the coconut.

2 Slice the cake into two thick layers so that each has the
same rectangular shape as the ice cream.

3 Cut the pineapple into triangles or quarters, cutting it over
the cake to catch any drips. On a baking sheet, arrange the fruit
on top of one slice of cake. Top with the ice cream and then
the second layer of cake.

4 Spread the meringue over the cake and ice cream, and bake
in the oven for 5–7 minutes, or until turning golden. Serve
immediately, topped with fruit.

Cook's Tips
• *Do not use soft-scoop ice cream for this dessert as it will
soften too quickly when heated in the oven.*
• *When covering the cake and ice cream with the meringue,
spread it carefully to ensure that no part of the pudding
underneath is exposed, or the ice cream will melt in the oven.*

Summer Fruit Brioche

Scooped-out individual
brioches make perfect
containers for the fruity
filling in this stylish but
simple dessert. If small
brioches are not available,
serve the fruit on slices cut
from a large brioche. Any
summer fruits can be used in
this dessert – try
raspberries, sliced peaches,
nectarines, apricots, or pitted
cherries. Serve with single
cream poured over.

Serves 4
300g/11oz/2½ cups small ripe
   strawberries, halved
30ml/2 tbsp caster
   (superfine) sugar
115g/4oz/⅔ cup raspberries
4 individual brioches

Preparation: 4 minutes; Cooking: 2–3 minutes

1 Put the strawberries in a pan with the sugar and add 60ml/
4 tbsp water. Heat very gently for about 1 minute, until the
strawberries are softened but still keep their shape. Remove
the pan from the heat, stir in the raspberries lightly and carefully
and leave for a couple of minutes to cool.

2 Preheat the grill (broiler). Slice the tops off the brioches
and use a teaspoon to scoop out their centres, leaving a
1cm/½in-thick case. Lightly toast them, turning once and
watching them carefully, as they will brown very quickly.

3 Place the hot toasted brioches on plates and pile the warm
fruit mixture into them. Add plenty of juice to saturate the
brioches and allow it to flood the plates. Place any extra fruit
on the plates, around the brioches, and serve immediately.

Variations
• *Use bought meringue shells instead of brioche cases. Let the
berry fruit mixture cool before spooning it into the shells, and
serve with whipped cream.*
• *Instead of poaching the berries lightly in a syrup made from
sugar and water, use raspberry jam, melting it with a little
water and a dash of lemon juice.*

Baked Alaska Energy 667kcal/2808kJ; Protein 10.8g; Carbohydrate 104.6g, of which sugars 93.9g; Fat 25.7g, of which saturates 9.8g; Cholesterol 33mg; Calcium 215mg; Fibre 2.3g; Sodium 317mg.
Fruit Brioche Energy 340kcal/1431kJ; Protein 5.1g; Carbohydrate 57.5g, of which sugars 41g; Fat 11.5g, of which saturates 6.4g; Cholesterol 0mg; Calcium 55mg; Fibre 2.2g; Sodium 291mg.

Summer Berries in Warm Sabayon Glaze

This luxurious combination consists of summer berries under a light and fluffy sauce flavoured with liqueur. The topping is lightly grilled to form a crisp, caramel crust.

Serves 4

450g/1lb/4 cups mixed summer berries, or soft fruit

4 egg yolks
50g/2oz/¼ cup vanilla sugar or caster (superfine) sugar
120ml/4fl oz/½ cup liqueur, such as Cointreau, Kirsch or Grand Marnier, or a white dessert wine
a little icing (confectioners') sugar, sifted, and mint leaves, to decorate (optional)

Preparation: 9 minutes; Cooking: 2 minutes

1 Arrange the fruit in four heatproof ramekins. Preheat the grill (broiler) using the maximum setting.

2 Put the egg yolks in a large heatproof bowl and add the sugar and liqueur or wine. Whisk lightly to mix. Place over a pan of hot water and whisk constantly until thick, fluffy and pale.

3 Pour equal quantities of the sabayon sauce over the fruit in each dish. Place under the grill for 1–2 minutes until just turning brown. Watch closely – the sabayon must not burn.

4 Dust the fruit with icing sugar and sprinkle with mint leaves just before serving, if you like. You could also add an extra splash of liqueur, or serve a glass of liqueur on the side.

> **Variations**
> • If you prefer to omit the alcohol, use grape, mango or apricot juice for flavouring instead of the liqueur.
> • Poached apricots can be used instead of the berry fruits, in which case toast some sliced almonds in a dry frying pan and use them to decorate the top of the desserts before serving. Hazelnuts could be used instead.

Fresh Summer Berries with Coffee Sabayon

For a light and deliciously refreshing finale, serve a platter of fresh summer fruit with a fluffy coffee sauce, which has the added advantage of being delightfully easy to make.

Serves 6

900g/2lb/6–8 cups mixed summer berries such as raspberries, blueberries and strawberries (hulled and halved, if large)

5 egg yolks
75g/3oz/scant ½ cup caster (superfine) sugar
50ml/2fl oz/¼ cup brewed coffee
30ml/2 tbsp coffee liqueur, such as Tia Maria, Kahlúa or Toussaint
strawberry or mint leaves, to decorate (optional)
30ml/2 tbsp icing (confectioners') sugar, to dust

Preparation: 3 minutes; Cooking: 4 minutes

1 Arrange the mixed summer berries on a serving platter or individual plates and decorate with strawberry or mint leaves, if you like. Dust with icing sugar.

2 Whisk the egg yolks and caster sugar in a bowl over a pan of simmering water until the mixture begins to thicken.

3 Gradually add the coffee and liqueur, pouring in a thin, continuous stream and whisking all the time.

4 Continue whisking until the sauce is thick and fluffy. Spoon into a wide-mouthed jug (pitcher) and serve warm, or allow to cool, whisking occasionally, and serve cold with the fresh mixed summer berries.

> **Cook's Tip**
> Ensure that the water doesn't get too hot when making the sauce, or it may curdle.

Berries in Glaze Energy 235kcal/984kJ; Protein 3.9g; Carbohydrate 27.1g, of which sugars 27.1g; Fat 5.6g, of which saturates 1.6g; Cholesterol 202mg; Calcium 48mg; Fibre 1.3g; Sodium 18mg.
Berries with Coffee Energy 219kcal/919kJ; Protein 3.9g; Carbohydrate 29.7g, of which sugars 29.7g; Fat 5.6g, of which saturates 1.6g; Cholesterol 202mg; Calcium 50mg; Fibre 1.2g; Sodium 20mg.

Tropical Fruit Gratin

This out-of-the-ordinary gratin is strictly for grown-ups. A colourful combination of fruit is topped with a simple sabayon before being flashed under the grill. The contrast between the hot, creamy topping and the cool, juicy fruit is the secret of its undeniable success.

Serves 4
2 tamarillos
1/2 sweet pineapple
1 ripe mango
175g/6oz/1 1/2 cups blackberries
120ml/4fl oz/1/2 cup sparkling
  white wine
115g/4oz/1/2 cup caster
  (superfine) sugar
6 egg yolks

Preparation: 8 minutes; Cooking: 10 minutes

1 Cut each tamarillo in half lengthways, then into thick slices. Cut the rind and core from the pineapple and take spiral slices off the outside to remove the eyes. Cut the flesh into chunks. Peel the mango and cut the flesh from the stone (pit) in slices.

2 Divide all the fruit, including the blackberries, among four 14cm/5 1/2in gratin dishes set on a baking sheet and set aside. Heat the wine and sugar in a pan until the sugar has dissolved. Bring to the boil and cook for 5 minutes.

3 Put the egg yolks in a large heatproof bowl. Place the bowl over a pan of simmering water and whisk until pale. Slowly pour on the hot sugar syrup, whisking all the time, until the mixture thickens. Preheat the grill (broiler).

4 Spoon the mixture over the fruit. Place the baking sheet holding the dishes on a low shelf under the hot grill until the topping is golden. Serve the gratin hot.

> **Variation**
> *Boiling drives off the alcohol in the wine, but children do not always appreciate the flavour. Substitute orange juice if making the gratin for them. White grape juice or pineapple juice would also work well.*

Chocolate & Orange Pancakes

Flip for these fabulous baby pancakes in a rich creamy orange liqueur sauce.

Serves 4
115g/4oz/1 cup self-raising
  (self-rising) flour
30ml/2 tbsp unsweetened
  cocoa powder
2 eggs
50g/2oz plain (semisweet)
  chocolate, broken into squares
200ml/7fl oz/scant 1 cup milk
finely grated rind of 1 orange

30ml/2 tbsp orange juice
butter or oil for frying
60ml/4 tbsp chocolate curls,
  for sprinkling

For the sauce
2 large oranges
30ml/2 tbsp unsalted
  (sweet) butter
45ml/3 tbsp light muscovado
  (brown) sugar
250ml/8fl oz/1 cup crème fraîche
30ml/2 tbsp Grand Marnier
chocolate curls, to decorate

Preparation: 6–8 minutes; Cooking: 12–14 minutes

1 Sift the flour and cocoa into a bowl and make a well in the centre. Add the eggs and beat well, gradually incorporating the surrounding dry ingredients to make a smooth batter.

2 Mix the chocolate and milk in a pan. Heat gently until the chocolate has melted, then beat into the batter until smooth and bubbly. Stir in the orange rind and juice.

3 Heat a large heavy frying pan and grease it. Drop large spoonfuls of batter on to the hot surface, leaving room for spreading. When the pancakes are lightly browned underneath and bubbly on top, flip them over to cook the other side. Slide on to a plate and keep hot while making more.

4 Make the sauce. Grate the rind of 1 orange into a bowl and set aside. Peel both oranges, taking care to remove all the pith, then slice the flesh fairly thinly. Heat the butter and sugar in a wide, shallow pan over a low heat, stirring until the sugar dissolves. Stir in the crème fraîche and heat gently. Heat the pancakes and orange slices in the sauce for 1–2 minutes, then spoon over the liqueur. Sprinkle with the reserved orange rind. Scatter over the chocolate curls and serve.

Gratin Energy 300kcal/1270kJ; Protein 6.2g; Carbohydrate 52.8g, of which sugars 52.7g; Fat 8.7g, of which saturates 2.4g; Cholesterol 302mg; Calcium 119mg; Fibre 4.6g; Sodium 22mg.
Pancakes Energy 752kcal/3131kJ; Protein 12.1g; Carbohydrate 58.1g, of which sugars 35.5g; Fat 53.2g, of which saturates 27g; Cholesterol 185mg; Calcium 282mg; Fibre 3.9g; Sodium 304mg.

Syrupy Brioche Slices with Vanilla Ice Cream

Keep a few individual brioche buns in the freezer to make this super dessert. For a slightly tarter taste, use finely grated lemon rind and juice instead of orange rind. For an everyday version of this simple dessert, use sliced currant buns – hot cross buns are an excellent vehicle for the spicy orange syrup – or even slices of raisin bread or fruity date loaf.

Serves 4
butter, for greasing
finely grated rind and juice of 1 orange, such as Navelina or blood orange
50g/2oz/¼ cup caster (superfine) sugar
90ml/6 tbsp water
1.5ml/¼ tsp ground cinnamon
4 brioche buns
15ml/1 tbsp icing (confectioners') sugar
400ml/14fl oz/1⅔ cups vanilla ice cream

Preparation: 4 minutes; Cooking: 9–10 minutes

1 Lightly grease a gratin dish and set aside. Put the orange rind and juice, sugar, water and cinnamon in a heavy pan. Heat gently, stirring constantly, until the sugar has dissolved, then boil rapidly, without stirring, for 2 minutes, until the mixture has thickened and is syrupy.

2 Remove the orange syrup from the heat and pour it into a shallow heatproof dish. Preheat the grill (broiler). Cut each brioche vertically into three thick slices. Dip one side of each slice in the hot syrup and arrange in the gratin dish, syrupy sides down. Reserve the remaining syrup. Grill (broil) the brioche under medium heat until lightly toasted.

3 Using tongs, turn the brioche slices over and dust well with icing sugar. Grill for about 3 minutes more, or until they are just beginning to caramelize around the edges.

4 Transfer the hot brioche to serving plates and top with scoops of vanilla ice cream. Spoon the remaining syrup over them and serve immediately.

Passion Fruit Soufflés

If you shun soufflés because you imagine them to be difficult, try these delightfully easy desserts based on bought custard. They are guaranteed to rise every time.

Serves 4
softened butter, for greasing
200ml/7fl oz/scant 1 cup ready-made fresh custard
3 passion fruit
2 egg whites

Preparation: 3–4 minutes; Cooking: 8–10 minutes

1 Preheat the oven to 200°C/400°F/Gas 6. Grease four 200ml/7fl oz/scant 1 cup ramekin dishes with the butter.

2 Pour the custard into a large mixing bowl. Cut the passion fruits in half. Using a teaspoon, carefully scrape out the seeds and juice from the halved passion fruit so that they drop straight on to the custard. Beat the mixture with a metal spoon until well combined, and set aside.

3 Whisk the egg whites in a clean, grease-free bowl until stiff, and fold a quarter of them into the custard.

4 Carefully fold the remaining egg whites into the custard, then spoon the mixture into the ramekin dishes. Place the dishes on a baking sheet and bake for 8–10 minutes, or until the soufflés are well risen. Serve immediately.

> **Variation**
> *Flavour the ready-made fresh custard with a little lemon curd, if you like. Lemon goes very well with passion fruit, and the slightly less sweet combination works well in these simple soufflés.*

> **Cook's Tip**
> *Run the tip of the spoon handle around the inner rim of the soufflé mixture in each ramekin before baking to ensure that the soufflé rises evenly when baked in the oven.*

Syrupy Brioche Energy 399kcal/1681kJ; Protein 8.5g; Carbohydrate 65.5g, of which sugars 42.5g; Fat 12g, of which saturates 7.2g; Cholesterol 25mg; Calcium 174mg; Fibre 1.3g; Sodium 252mg.
Passion Fruit Soufflés Energy 59kcal/249kJ; Protein 3.1g; Carbohydrate 8.8g, of which sugars 7.1g; Fat 1g, of which saturates 0g; Cholesterol 1mg; Calcium 48mg; Fibre 0.4g; Sodium 53mg.

Chocolate & Prune Bars

Wickedly self-indulgent and very easy to make, these fruity chocolate bars will keep for 2–3 days in the refrigerator – if they don't all get eaten as soon as they are ready. For an adult treat, soak the prunes in brandy before use.

Makes 12 bars
250g/9oz good quality
  milk chocolate
50g/2oz/¼ cup unsalted
  (sweet) butter
115g/4oz digestive biscuits
  (graham crackers)
115g/4oz/½ cup ready-to-eat
  prunes

Preparation: 4–5 minutes; Cooking: 0 minutes; Chill ahead

1 Break the chocolate into small pieces and place in a heatproof bowl. Add the butter and melt in the microwave on High for 1–2 minutes. Stir to mix and set aside. (Alternatively, place the chocolate pieces and butter in a bowl over a pan of gently simmering water and leave until melted, stirring frequently.)

2 Put the biscuits in a plastic bag and seal, then bash into small pieces with a rolling pin. Alternatively, break up the biscuits in a food processor but do not let them become too fine. Use the pulse button or process in short bursts.

3 Roughly chop the prunes and stir into the melted chocolate with the biscuits. Spoon the mixture into a 20cm/8in square cake tin (pan) and smooth out any lumps with the back of the spoon. Chill for 1–2 hours until set. Remove the cake from the refrigerator and, using a sharp knife, cut into 12 bars.

Variations
• Use dark (bittersweet) chocolate instead of milk chocolate. Fruit and nut chocolate makes for particularly rich-tasting bars.
• Any firm sweet biscuit (cookie) can be used. Gingernuts (gingersnaps) are delicious, especially if preserved or candied ginger is added with or instead of the prunes.
• Substitute dried apricots or peaches for the prunes. This variation works well with orange-flavoured chocolate.

Cinnamon & Orange Tuiles

The aroma of cinnamon and orange evokes a feeling of Christmas. These chocolate-dipped tuiles are perfect for festive occasions.

Makes 15
2 egg whites
90g/3½ oz/½ cup caster
  (superfine) sugar
7.5ml/1½ tsp ground cinnamon

finely grated rind of 1 orange
50g/2oz/½ cup plain
  (all-purpose) flour
75g/3oz/6 tbsp butter, melted

For the dipping chocolate
75g/3oz Belgian plain
  (semisweet) chocolate
45ml/3 tbsp milk
75–90ml/5–6 tbsp double
  (heavy) or whipping cream

Preparation: 4 minutes; Cooking: 12–14 minutes; Make ahead

1 Preheat the oven to 200°C/400°F/Gas 6. Line two very large baking trays with baking parchment.

2 Whisk the egg whites until softly peaking, then whisk in the sugar until smooth and glossy. Add the cinnamon and orange rind, sift over the flour and fold in with the melted butter. When well blended, stir in 15ml/1 tbsp of recently boiled water.

3 Place 4–5 teaspoons of the mixture on each tray, well apart. Flatten out and bake, one tray at a time, for 6–7 minutes until just turning golden. Cool for a few seconds then remove from the tray with a fish slice or metal spatula and immediately roll around the handle of a wooden spoon. Place on a rack to cool.

4 To make the dipping chocolate, melt the chocolate slowly in the milk until smooth, then stir in the cream. Dip one or both ends of the biscuits in the chocolate and cool.

Cook's Tip
If you haven't made these before, cook only one or two at a time until you get the hang of it. If they harden too quickly to allow you time to roll them, return the baking sheet to the oven for a few seconds, then try rolling them again.

Chocolate Bars Energy 197kcal/826kJ; Protein 2.5g; Carbohydrate 21.7g, of which sugars 16.4g; Fat 11.8g, of which saturates 6.8g; Cholesterol 18mg; Calcium 59mg; Fibre 0.9g; Sodium 102mg.
Cinnamon Tuiles Energy 125kcal/523kJ; Protein 1.2g; Carbohydrate 12.3g, of which sugars 9.7g; Fat 8.3g, of which saturates 5.2g; Cholesterol 18mg; Calcium 17mg; Fibre 0.2g; Sodium 42mg.

All Butter Cookies

These biscuits or cookies are known as refrigerator biscuits as the mixture is chilled until it is firm enough to cut neatly into thin biscuits. The dough can be frozen and when thawed enough to slice, can be freshly baked, but do allow a little extra cooking time.

Makes 28–30
275g/10oz/2½ cups plain (all-purpose) flour
200g/7oz/scant 1 cup unsalted (sweet) butter
90g/3½ oz/scant 1 cup icing (confectioners') sugar, plus extra for dusting
10ml/2 tsp vanilla extract

Preparation: 5–7 minutes; Cooking: 8–10 minutes; Chilling: 1 hour

1 Put the flour in a food processor. Add the butter and process until the mixture resembles coarse breadcrumbs. Add the icing sugar and vanilla, and process until the mixture comes together to form a dough. Knead lightly and shape into a thick sausage, 30cm/12in long and 5cm/2in in diameter. Wrap and chill for at least 1 hour, until firm.

2 Preheat the oven to 200°C/400°F/Gas 6. Grease two baking sheets. Using a sharp knife, cut 5mm/¼ in thick slices from the dough and space them slightly apart on the baking sheet.

3 Bake for 8–10 minutes, alternating the position of the baking sheets in the oven halfway through cooking, if necessary, until the biscuits are cooked evenly and have just turned pale golden around the edges. Leave for 5 minutes, then transfer to a wire rack to cool. Serve dusted with icing sugar.

Cook's Tips
• *These cookies do not spread much when baked, so can be spaced fairly close together on the baking sheets. Leave a little room between them, though, or they will be more difficult to lift off once they have cooled slightly.*
• *Transfer the cooked cookies to the wire rack with a spatula. They will still be softish at this stage but will firm up on cooling.*

Anglesey Shortbread

Originating in Aberffraw, a village on Anglesey, these biscuits are called 'Teisen Berffro' in Welsh. They are made by pressing the dough into a queen scallop shell prior to baking. They do, of course, taste just as good without the marking.

Makes 12
100g/3½ oz/½ cup butter, softened
50g/2oz/¼ cup caster (superfine) sugar, plus extra for sprinkling
150g/5½ oz/1¼ cups plain (all-purpose) flour

Preparation: 6–7 minutes; Cooking: 10 minutes

1 Preheat the oven to 200°C/400°F/Gas 6. Line a baking sheet with baking parchment.

2 Put the butter and sugar into a bowl and beat until light and fluffy. Sift the flour over and stir it in until the mixture can be gathered into a ball of soft dough.

3 Knead the dough, working it back and forth so that the warmth of your hand keeps the dough soft and pliable. Divide and shape it into 12 balls.

4 Sprinkle the inside of a scallop shell with sugar, and gently press a ball of dough into it, spreading it evenly so the shell is filled. Invert on to the paper-lined sheet, pressing it down to flatten the base and to mark it with the impression of the shell.

5 Lift the shell off, carefully prising out the dough. Alternatively, press or roll the dough balls into plain biscuits (cookies) measuring about 5cm/2in across.

6 Put into the hot oven and cook for about 10 minutes until set. Traditionally, they should not be allowed to brown, but they look very attractive and taste delicious with crisp golden edges.

7 Sprinkle with a little extra sugar, transfer to a wire rack and leave to cool completely.

Shortbread Energy 121kcal/506kJ; Protein 1.2g; Carbohydrate 14.1g, of which sugars 4.6g; Fat 7g, of which saturates 4.4g; Cholesterol 18mg; Calcium 21mg; Fibre 0.4g; Sodium 51mg.
Cookies Energy 84kcal/350kJ; Protein 0.8g; Carbohydrate 9.6g, of which sugars 3.3g; Fat 4.9g, of which saturates 3.1g; Cholesterol 12mg; Calcium 14mg; Fibre 0.3g; Sodium 36mg.

Index